STAND TALL

Teacher's Manual & DVD

GRADES 4–6

To Abe, Bobby, Doug, and Rob.

STAND TALL

Teacher's Manual & DVD

GRADES 4–6

Lessons That Teach Respect and Prevent Bullying

SUZANNE W. PECK

Foreword by Jane Close Conoley

CORWIN
A SAGE Company

CORWIN
A SAGE Company

FOR INFORMATION:

Corwin
A SAGE Company
2455 Teller Road
Thousand Oaks, California 91320
(800) 233-9936
Fax: (800) 417-2466
www.corwin.com

SAGE Publications Ltd.
1 Oliver's Yard
55 City Road
London EC1Y 1SP
United Kingdom

SAGE Publications India Pvt. Ltd.
B 1/I 1 Mohan Cooperative Industrial Area
Mathura Road, New Delhi 110 044
India

SAGE Publications Asia-Pacific Pte. Ltd.
33 Pekin Street #02-01
Far East Square
Singapore 048763

Acquisitions Editor: Jessica Allan
Associate Editor: Allison Scott
Editorial Assistant: Lisa Whitney
Developmental Editor: Nancy Oster
Production Editor: Cassandra Margaret Seibel
Copy Editor: Sarah J. Duffy
Typesetter: C&M Digitals (P) Ltd.
Proofreader: Lawrence W. Baker
Indexer: Scott Smiley
Cover Designer: Scott Van Atta
Permissions Editor: Karen Ehrmann

Copyright © 2012 by Suzanne W. Peck

Printed in the United States of America.

Library of Congress Cataloging-in-Publication Data

Peck, Suzanne W.

Stand tall teacher's manual & DVD, Grades 4–6: lessons that teach respect and prevent bullying/Suzanne W. Peck; foreword by Jane Close Conoley.

p. cm.
Includes bibliographical references and index.

ISBN 978-1-4522-0529-8 (pbk.)
ISBN 978-1-4522-4105-0 (pbk w/DVD)

1. Multicultural education—Audio-visual aids. 2. Bullying in schools—Prevention—Audio-visual aids. 3. Multiculturalism—Study and teaching (Elementary)—Audio-visual aids. 4. Education, Elementary—Audio-visual aids. I. Title.

LC1099.P43 2012
370.117—dc23   2011040856

This book is printed on acid-free paper.

SUSTAINABLE FORESTRY INITIATIVE

Certified Chain of Custody
Promoting Sustainable Forestry
www.sfiprogram.org
SFI-01268

SFI label applies to text stock

12 13 14 15 16 10 9 8 7 6 5 4 3 2 1

Contents

Foreword

At my first meeting with Suzanne Peck, she introduced the idea of applying the expertise she had gained through a successful career in corporate training to elementary and middle school classrooms. I was both impressed by her passion for social justice and a little concerned that her corporate experience might not translate easily to children and into busy classrooms. Any initial doubts vanished, however, over the months that followed. She dug into the experiences of teachers and children, families and school administrators. She met with university faculty experts and developed creative approaches to make her messages of tolerance, celebration of differences, and personal empowerment vital and engaging.

The final product, STAND TALL, is an authentic set of resources for educators. Suzanne illustrates her respect for classroom teachers in so many ways through this work. For example, she gives them critical information about the law. How refreshing to share this with educators on the front line. Suzanne has thought through what teachers need in order to successfully accomplish each STAND TALL objective. She prepares them conceptually and lists the exact materials and parent communications that will support youngsters' success. She also explicitly links the skills learned through STAND TALL with prevailing state academic content and process standards.

The work is a masterpiece of integration. Youngsters who engage with the activities outlined in the book will improve their written and verbal communication skills, gain experiences with meaningful collaboration, learn about themselves and their places in the world (family and community), and develop skills and attitudes for personal growth and peer success.

We may have once thought that being bullied or harassed was a rite of passage to be endured by all children. We now know that all those involved with intolerance and aggression are scarred by the experiences. These are not just personal hurts; they represent a failure of community to nurture all members with care and respect. Intolerance is not new or localized to a few arenas. It's time, however, to speak up, work with others, and act to eradicate it. STAND TALL provides the tools to make this happen.

Jane Close Conoley, PhD
Dean and Professor
Gevirtz Graduate School of Education
University of California Santa Barbara

Acknowledgments

When STAND TALL was just embryonic, three legendary leaders encouraged me to pursue its vision: Sara Miller McCune, Rabbi Arthur Gross-Schaefer, and Marilyn Gevirtz. As mentors and spiritual sounding boards, their belief that I could create a program to have a transformative impact in schools across the country stoked my fire.

I set out with the goal of preventing bullying and—equally important—giving kids positive skills to build respect and deal with disrespect. Diving in for 18 months, I've been fortunate to have many of the best academic, educational, and legal minds as contributors and collaborators.

At the head of the academic class, Jane Close Conoley, dean and professor at the University of California Santa Barbara (UCSB), Gevirtz Graduate School of Education, has inspired me, advised me, and opened doors from my first outline to this finished product. Also at UCSB, Patricia Marin, John Yun, Judith Green, Michael Young, Jackie Reid, Rich Applebaum, and Beth Yeager generously shared ideas and energy along the way.

Growing up with a judge for a dad and a judge for a sister, I appreciate the importance and complexity of legal mandates and liabilities. It surprised me to learn how few teachers know the civil rights and harassment laws they are responsible for implementing. I'm extremely grateful for the technical assistance of three outstanding attorneys as I prepared the plain-English legal summaries: Sara N. Berman, Suzanne Taylor, and James M. Wood, all with the U.S. Department of Education, Office for Civil Rights.

Signing on early with Corwin, an enormous body of educational knowledge and professional development resources became easily accessible to me. Corwin authors and educators who have experience in the areas of bullying, teaching methods, equity, and diversity helped to shape this program. Mike Soules, Jessica Allan, Dan Alpert, and Anthony Paular contributed a world of creative ideas, introductions, and stacks of wonderful books. You'll see two of my favorite Corwin experts in the "Teacher's Introduction" video segment: Walter Roberts, professor of counselor education at Minnesota State University, and Ronald Mah, educator and family therapist, provided practical advice and the latest expertise on bullying. Speaking of the video, special thanks go to John Klein for his artful, precise, brilliant, and collaborative editing of the video version of STAND TALL.

I've been privileged to cofacilitate hundreds of training sessions with Charles Lee over the past 25 years. In addition to his technical expertise in civil rights, diversity, and harassment, Charles is a world-class pro at teaching techniques. His PhD dissertation was on the use of simulations and games as educative interventions in multicultural training. So when I decided to use improvisational theater games in STAND TALL, Charles was tremendously helpful. His teaching experience in Georgia, New Jersey, New York, Ohio, and Turkey provided a rich perspective on ways to have a transformative impact.

Speaking of improv theater games, three stellar actors and workshop facilitators with The Second City contributed to STAND TALL. The Second City is the largest school of improv in the world, and they have found improv to be a highly effective instructional tool for students to develop skills in creative problem solving and collaboration. Collaborating with Rob Lindley, Niki Lindgren, and Jennifer Hoyt was simply amazing.

Teachers, counselors, principals, school superintendents, parents, and community leaders from across the country shared stories, advice, and lessons learned. Special thanks to Bev Abrams, Marie Alviz, Barbara Ben-Horin, Theresa Bothman, Kevin Bradley, Deborah Brown, Joe Bruzzese, Peggy Buffington, Sylvia Camiel, Jennifer Cannon, Walter Claudio, Steve Cohen, Randee Disraeli, Laura Donner, Clair Durkes, Kate Ford, Sid Ganis, Nina Gelman-Gans, Jeff and Karen Genest, Robert Gnaizda, Laurie Gross, Wendy Kanter, Judy Karin, Hilary Dole Klein, Tim Kochis, Lucius Lamar, Gary and Vicky Linker, Lisa Lucas, Ann Manikas, Joe Medellin, Judy Meisel, Sonia Morosin, Linda Ng, Ann Noel, Adrienne O'Donnell, Lily Passell, Marianne Partridge, Joan Peters, Ellen and Rob Raede, Laura Roberts, Susan Rose, Adele Rosen, Dana Sadan, Jane Santos, Lynda Schwartz, Cyndi Silverman, Cheri Steinkellner, Rhoda Sweeney, Michael Tapia, Mae Cendaña Torlakson, Tom Torlakson, Violet Torres, Marjorie Troob,

Cynthia Wang, Judi Weisbart, Layne Wheeler, Penelope Wong, and others whose names are on scraps of paper buried in my research files.

I'm extremely grateful for the help of Nancy Oster, developmental editor for this book. The compendium of resources, lesson plans, and careful editing reflect her brilliant touch. Nancy is a writer, healthcare activist, Internet expert, educator, and the author of *Making Informed Medical Decisions*. On top of all that, she's a chef, so we enjoyed wonderful snacks as we worked.

In addition to the dozens of confidential interviews I conducted with kids in public schools, private schools, charter schools, and home-school environments, my three 11-year-old nieces—Joie, Emily, and Rachel—were great reality checks for what works in New York, Illinois, and California classrooms. Big hugs to all, and may you always stand tall.

About the Author

Suzanne W. Peck, educator, author, and consultant, designs and leads training programs for culturally diverse audiences of all ages. After public school teaching assignments in Chicago, Illinois, and Lexington, Massachusetts, she began leading teacher training programs with Interaction Associates, in San Francisco, California, and teaching courses in education and communication studies at Dominican University, in San Rafael, California.

Teacher training programs led to corporate training programs, and Suzanne joined Towers Perrin (now Towers Watson), a management consulting firm with 14,000 consultants in offices around the world. She founded and led the company's training practice, with a technical focus on equal employment opportunity, diversity, and harassment. She became a principal and led the firm's human resources and communication line of business.

Suzanne has worked with Fortune 500 companies to manage diversity and change for more than 30 years. At organizations from McDonald's to Disney to University of Chicago Hospitals to GE, she has partnered with executives to develop educational programs and create team approaches both nationally and internationally.

In addition to consulting, Suzanne has taught diversity within Northwestern University's Media Management Center, an executive education program led by faculty of the Kellogg School of Management and the Medill School of Journalism. She also serves on the Dean's Council of the University of California Santa Barbara Gevirtz Graduate School of Education. A sought-after public speaker and trainer, she has won many awards for creative excellence in communication and training programs, including from the International Association of Business Communicators, the Human Resources Management Association, and the U.S. Industrial Film and Video Festival.

Suzanne coauthored *RUFF: A Lost Dog Tale, 5 Great Strategies to Manage Change at Work and Beyond* with Penelope Wong. She participated in the development of *I'm in Charge,* a health care consumer-assertiveness education program used by more than one million employees in 400 companies; *Expect the Best,* starring Phylicia and Ahmad Rashad; *How to Make Meetings Work,* now in its ninth printing; and *Boomerang,* an equal employment opportunity training program used by half of the Fortune 500.

Introduction

Education, at best, is ecstatic. At its best, its most effective, its most unfettered, the moment of learning is a moment of delight. When joy is absent, the effectiveness of the learning process falls and falls until the human being is operating hesitantly, grudgingly, fearfully at only a tiny fraction of his potential.

George Leonard, *Education and Ecstasy*

Those moments of learning, those moments of delight . . . that's what it's all about. The impact of a positive, safe, respectful learning environment on students' academic achievement is visible, and it's a joy to behold.

When kids are happy at school, they learn more. You've seen this. And while the challenges you face every day are all too real, STAND TALL offers the tools to implement a social and emotional classroom dynamic that helps students achieve at full potential.

With seven quick chapters and four evocative videos, STAND TALL builds three core competencies:

1. RESPECT for individual differences

Everyone deserves to be treated with respect at school, and there are relevant civil rights and harassment laws that teachers must understand and implement. But even if these laws didn't exist, to quote George Leonard again, "the effectiveness of the learning process falls and falls" when kids feel disrespected.

2. DISCUSSION to further understanding

Listening and learning from others with different perspectives is a critical 21st-century skill that kids need to learn. STAND TALL is structured to build teamwork, conflict resolution skills, and a strong learning community.

3. ACTION that transforms behavior

Speaking up when offended or disrespected is an important skill, and children in Grades 4–6 are at the most teachable age to develop it. Kids need to learn how to respond in constructive, effective, and safe ways when they experience or observe disrespect.

STAND TALL is based on sage advice from leading experts and my more than 30 years of teaching people about diversity, harassment, equal employment opportunity, and workforce change— developing techniques first used in front of fifth and sixth graders at Edward Jenner Elementary School, in Chicago. My students since then have been Fortune 500 business executives and folks who work in steel mills. My "classrooms" have been in Troy, Alabama; New York City; Oak Brook, Illinois; Monroe, Louisiana; Cincinnati, Ohio; Los Angeles, California; and just about everywhere in between. Some learning took place in perfectly outfitted conference rooms, and some in trailers that doubled as employee break rooms. The topics we covered are very close to what you'll see in STAND TALL.

One of the skills I've *always* emphasized is how and when to speak up if offended. On thousands of postsession evaluation sheets, the most frequent comment by far has been about the value of learning how to handle disrespect: "I wish I would've learned this a long time ago." "Using this skill could've helped me avoid a couple of really major fiascos." "They should teach this to kids when they're young." That last one really got me.

We shouldn't need national headlines about deadly bullying and student suicides to focus on respect for differences. But this truly has been a wake-up call. STAND TALL is a reply to violence . . . the violence of bullying and harassment.

> *This will be our reply to violence: to make music more intensely, more beautifully, more devotedly than ever before.*
>
> Leonard Bernstein

You can use STAND TALL to prevent harassment *and* strengthen the learning environment. Your students will enjoy the videos and classroom exercises, while building skills and tools that are critical for creating a strong classroom community.

This book includes a short and sweet summary of the legal responsibility to maintain a classroom environment free of harassment based on race, color, national origin, sex, religion, gender stereotype, or disability. Very few teachers have had any instruction regarding hostile environment, protected classes, prompt corrective action, or liability issues. This is must-know information for all teachers. But even if it were not the law, teachers know that when kids are hurt or angry about name-calling, harassment, and bullying, they don't focus on schoolwork.

STAND TALL is devotedly positive. Teachers create amazing learning environments, often despite humongous challenges. Woven throughout this book are wonderful stories that inspire action, best practices, and practical suggestions to link STAND TALL lessons to curriculum standards for social studies, health, language arts, math, and art.

We know that kids achieve more academically in a positive learning environment. And, as Bill Gates reminds us, "We know that kids can change by the way teachers act." One of the most critical factors that impact students' academic achievement is whether they've had a good teacher. STAND TALL is a tool you can use to build a skill your students will use throughout their lives.

So it's my hope that STAND TALL will help you create a powerfully positive learning environment in which all students feel respected—and know how to handle disrespect when it rears its ugly head.

1

How to Use STAND TALL in Your Classroom

Getting Started

The STAND TALL approach won't take a lot of prep time, and it's an easy fit with curriculum standards. All it takes is these three steps:

1. Watch all four segments of the STAND TALL video/DVD:
   - "Teacher's Introduction," featuring four experts with practical advice to prevent bullying [9 minutes]
   - "Let's Talk About RESPECT for Individual Differences," part of the first classroom module [10 minutes]
   - "Let's Have a Constructive DISCUSSION," part of the second classroom module [7 minutes]
   - "Let's Talk About ACTION and Options," part of the third classroom module [8 minutes]

2. Review the corresponding chapters for instructional materials that build on video segments 2, 3, and 4. Each classroom module provides ways to link the key learning points to your curriculum, sample lesson plans, and tools to develop the three competencies.

3. Read Chapter 2, "Your LEGAL Responsibilities and School Policy," then review your current school policy on harassment and bullying. School policies across the country are literally all over the map on critical issues such as disciplinary measures and physical contact. So read your policy carefully, and ask for clarification if anything is vague or confusing. You may teach in a district with a "Don't Say Gay" policy, or maybe your state requires public schools to teach gay and lesbian history. California, which recently passed a law making it the first state to require public schools to teach gay and lesbian history, already requires schools to teach students about the contributions of other minority groups and women. This new law is designed to combat bullying. Laws in many states and policies in many districts are changing to address concerns over bullying, school safety, and liability. So stay current and know your legal responsibilities, including the fact that you have **personal liability**.

Methodology

Each of the three classroom modules follows this instructional design:

Watch a Short Video

This sets the stage in 8 or 9 minutes—in a way that's both fun and interesting for your students. They will see kids their age sharing stories, discussing examples, and generating a range of constructive solutions to challenges. The film shows students working with Jennifer Hoyt, an actor from the famed Second City improvisational troupe, on alternative ways to respond in different situations. Jennifer leads the kids through theater games that illuminate our three competencies: RESPECT, DISCUSSION, and ACTION. The videos will spark great discussions and motivation to work on these skills.

Talk About It

Try a two-step process. First off, have your class engage in small-group discussions so everyone gets a chance to participate. We provide scaffold questions to help your students analyze the video examples and focus on the key learning points. We recommend 5 to 10 minutes for these discussions. The topics emphasize solutions. They focus on respect for differences and ways to respond to disrespect. Building on the small-group discussions, you can summarize and post the key learning points for the whole class—using their own words, and with agreements they've created.

Practice the Skill

Each module includes a STAND TALL lesson plan to increase student awareness and stimulate more discussion. The lesson plans link to curriculum standards in language arts, social studies, health, math, and art.

We have specifically targeted Grades 4–6. This level is an age that is extremely critical to formation of lifelong attitudes and behaviors about differences. A study by the University of California at Berkeley and the Anti-Defamation League found that "by the age of 12, children have already developed a complete set of stereotypes about every ethnic, racial, and religious group in society." Moreover, a national survey recently conducted by the Kaiser Family Foundation (2011) and Nickelodeon, "Talking With Kids About Tough Issues," found that 74% of 8- to 11-year-old students said that teasing and bullying occur at their schools. You may not see it, but it's there and requires our ongoing attention.

So don't just show the films and then put this program on the shelf. Please, please, please keep talking about respect for differences, use the tools we provide, and check out the additional resources, books, and websites for ongoing education on each topic. Keep it alive. This is a skill that deserves ongoing discussion and reinforcement.

> "There is extensive evidence that drama provides opportunities to create and experiment with life-like conflicts, but which are made safe by being fictional. Emotions remain unthreatened and the participants are always in control. Students can explore an experience safely by pretending it is real while knowing it is fictional."
>
> Source: *Acting Against Bullying: Using Drama and Peer Teaching to Reduce Bullying,* John O'Toole and Bruce Burton, 2010.

Discussion Guidelines

Before showing each video module, spend a few minutes talking about ground rules and establishing agreements that will encourage good participation and constructive dialogue. The following is a sample list you can post. Note the acronym PLUS—be sure to emphasize that you want to have a positive discussion. Ask your students what else they think is important to encourage positive discussion and create a safe space where everyone feels free to contribute.

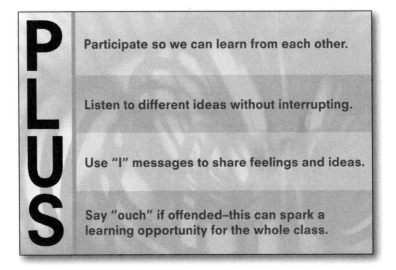

P Participate so we can learn from each other.

L Listen to different ideas without interrupting.

U Use "I" messages to share feelings and ideas.

S Say "ouch" if offended–this can spark a learning opportunity for the whole class.

Finding a Good Fit

- Choose one of the books suggested in Chapter 7 to read and discuss in class as a supplement to each module.
- Review Chapter 6, "STAND TALL With Your Community" for ways to involve parents, local businesses, and others in your extended community.
- Use the skills you are teaching with STAND TALL to meet core curriculum standards. You can meet standards in multiple areas, for example:

Language Arts Outcomes

- Listens carefully to what others have to say
- Recognizes stereotypes
- Uses writing to express and communicate thoughts and information to others

- Learns to gather and record information in the form of research
- Understands that some attitudes are communicated in a nonverbal way through body language, gestures, tone, and inflection

Social Studies Outcomes

- Learns the fundamental values of a constitutional democracy open to people of any ethnicity, race, religion, gender, and national origin
- Learns to respect human differences without discrimination
- Recognizes the benefits and challenges of diverse populations in the United States
- Recognizes American ideals of equal rights and equal justice
- Understands the importance of honesty, responsibility, and compassion in maintaining a healthy democracy
- Learns that the American population is composed of people from many cultures and countries who have come here for many different reasons
- Becomes familiar with the location of different countries and regions

Physical Education and Health Outcomes

- Participates in group activities that require cooperative behavior
- Recognizes and supports the differences in physical skills of all students
- Learns how to manage stress
- Identifies nonviolent ways to communicate feelings and respond to negative peer pressure and conflict
- Develops self-confidence
- Anticipates ways to prevent or solve problems
- Shows respect for others when working in a group

Art Outcomes

- Uses art to express feelings, situations, and consequences
- Uses graphs and diagrams to describe a situation

You get the picture. The skills you will be teaching in STAND TALL are entwined in basic curriculum standards in more than one subject area. For more examples of standards and benchmarks, check out the websites listed in Chapter 7.

Make Kids Heroes

Look for opportunities to reinforce respectful behaviors, constructive dialogue, speaking up for others, and resolving conflicts. Make heroes out of kids who STAND TALL! Describe their behavior in a specific way and express appreciation for their maturity, thoughtfulness, good communication skills, consideration, careful listening, collaborative problem solving, and learning from different perspectives. Focus on positive behaviors and visible results. Keep the dialogue going on the topic of respect throughout the school year.

Use positive psychology to help your kids STAND TALL. My favorite tool for this comes from *Positive Psychology and Family Therapy: Creative Techniques and Practical Tools for Guiding Change and Enhancing Growth*, by Professor Collie W. Conoley and Dean Jane Close Conoley (2009), of the University of California Santa Barbara Gevirtz Graduate School of Education. The Conoleys call it "punctuating the positive or focusing on strengths." Why is it so important for teachers to punctuate the positive? The Conoleys' research finds that positive focus on strengths is "critical to keep . . . energy high, motivation strong, and hopes elevated." So punctuate the positive every chance you get.

Figure 1.1　Benefits of Social and Emotional Learning

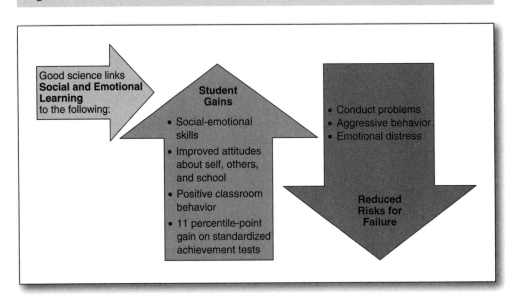

Source: Collaborative for Academic, Social, and Emotional Learning, 2011. Used with permission.

Help Kids Make Smart Choices

Do everything you can to create a positive learning environment; there will still be hurtful behavior. You can't always be there, but you can make sure that your students know how to respond in tough situations. Consider the potential impact of social media and 24/7 cyberbullying. In their book *Bullying Beyond the Schoolyard*, Sameer Hinduja and Justin Patchin (2009), professors at the University of Wisconsin and Florida Atlantic University, respectively, state forcefully, "Educators must convey to students that if they see or receive electronic content that mistreats or makes fun of another person, they should immediately contact an adult." Hinduja and Patchin provide excellent tools to prevent cyberbullying. You may think your students are a bit young for this, but why not start them off knowing how to make smart choices . . . just in case:

What Kids Should Do
If They Witness Cyberbullying

- Document what they see and when.
- Don't encourage the behavior.
- Don't forward hurtful messages.
- Don't laugh at inappropriate jokes.
- Don't condone the act just to fit in.
- Don't silently allow it to continue.
- Stand up for the victim.
- Tell an adult they trust.

Source: Hinduja & Patchin, 2009, p. 175.

2

Your LEGAL Responsibilities and School Policy

I don't know about you, but when I studied education in college, earned teaching certificates in two states, and taught in three, no one told me about the laws I was responsible for as a teacher. I've asked around to find out if somehow I just missed it. Here are a few responses I got from other teachers:

"I never had a class on the laws or any instruction about my legal responsibilities. Was I supposed to?"

"I don't know what the laws are, so I just hope I don't break any."

"I had a fabulous public school law class, but the laws have changed a lot since I was in school."

"It'd be good to know what's covered and what preventive things we can do."

Where Were You on October 26, 2010?

I was with Brian Williams. Well, actually, watching him report on the *NBC Nightly News* about a letter of monumental importance in the field of education. Brian said that "bullying is out of control," so the U.S. Department of Education's Office for Civil Rights (OCR) sent educators across the country a very detailed and urgent letter explaining their **legal duties to protect students from bullying and harassment** based on race, color, national origin, sex, disability, and religion. This important letter was sent to 15,000 school districts and 5,000 colleges and universities on that day.

You're not alone if you didn't read the 10-page single-spaced letter or immediately go to the Department of Education website to learn all about it. Your answer to the question about your whereabouts on that October 26 probably describes an extremely busy day teaching, then going home with a couple of hours' more work to squeeze in on top of a full plate of responsibilities on the home front. That leaves you with zero time to watch the *Nightly News* or surf the web for professional development. So you just might have missed hearing about this very important letter. I won't even ask you about the 19-page single-spaced April 4, 2011, letter sent to 15,000 schools by the OCR. It also provided "must know" legal information for all teachers. This one focused on school-based sexual harassment. The data are shocking.

Why Should You Care About These Laws?

We have an obligation to ensure that our schools are safe for all of our kids. Every single young person deserves the opportunity to learn and grow and achieve their potential, without having to worry about the constant threat of harassment.

—President Barack Obama (OCR, 2010b)

You play a critical role in creating and maintaining a classroom environment free of harassment. You are the key person to foster a positive and safe learning environment for maximum academic achievement. Still, we know there will be problems. While it may be tempting to refer a "problem" to the principal or your school counselor and think your job is mostly done, you still have responsibility for corrective and preventive action—and **personal liability** if a situation is not handled well. It's not someone else's responsibility.

What Should You Know?

Ignorance of the law is no excuse. You have a responsibility to understand and implement civil rights and harassment laws. There are federal, state, and local laws that apply, as well as your school policy. You need to know how harassment is defined under the law, how to prevent it, how to respond when you see it, and how to use the resources that are available for guidance. In this chapter I break it down to the top 10 questions I've heard from teachers and in hundreds of training classes on preventing harassment.

Ten questions may seem like a lot. So keep in mind that there are excellent resources available to you for ongoing guidance. I refer to some in this chapter and provide a more complete listing in Chapter 7.

And there's one more thing you must know: I am not a lawyer. I am not giving you legal advice. My goal is to make you aware of the federal laws related to school-based harassment and let you know where you can get specific guidance and more detailed information. This chapter gives you an overview and explains key terms you should know. Be sure to ask your principal or the person in your school district who is responsible for getting legal advice on these matters.

The OCR is an outstanding resource, staffed with attorneys in 12 regional offices around the country. This is a complicated and evolving area of the law, so it's good to know that resources are there for you.

Top 10 Questions

1. What Is Harassment?

Harassment is unwanted, offensive behavior directed at an individual or a group on the basis of race, color, sex, gender stereotype, national origin, religion, or disability. It can be verbal, visual, physical, relational, graphic, or electronic, including the use of cell phones and the Internet. It can be obvious or subtle. It can happen in a classroom, hallway, bathroom, library, playground, or on a school bus.

There's often a distinction made between harassment and bullying. Harassment is a legal term, and that's what we'll concentrate on here. Kids, though, often use the term *bullying,* which is a word they are more likely to understand. That's okay. Your school policy probably mentions both harassment and bullying. Rather than dwell on what is sometimes a false distinction, we will focus on the legal definition of harassment in this chapter.

Harassment is a form of illegal discrimination. School districts can be in violation of federal law when peer harassment based on race, color, national origin, sex, gender stereotype, religion, or disability is "sufficiently serious that it creates a hostile environment, and such harassment is encouraged, tolerated, not adequately addressed, or ignored by school employees" (OCR, 2010a).

I doubt that you would "encourage" harassment, but the way the laws address school employees who tolerate, ignore, or do not adequately address the harassment is another matter, one that is very important for you to understand. You do not want to tolerate, ignore, or fail to address harassment when you see it.

2. What Federal Laws Are Teachers Responsible for Implementing?

These are the federal regulations that apply:

- Title VI of the Civil Rights Act of 1964 prohibits discrimination on the basis of **race, color, and national origin**.
- Title IX of the Education Amendments of 1972 prohibits discrimination on the basis of **sex**, including nonconformity with gender stereotypes.
- Section 504 of the Rehabilitation Act of 1973 and Title II of the Americans with Disabilities Act of 1990 prohibit discrimination on the basis of **disability**.
- Title IV of the Civil Rights Act of 1964 prohibits discrimination on the basis of race, color, sex, gender stereotype, **religion,** or national origin by public elementary and secondary schools and public institutions of higher learning.

3. What State Laws Apply?

Some state laws specifically prohibit harassment on the basis of sexual orientation and other protected classes. As of this writing, 45 states have passed laws addressing harassment and bullying. Ask your principal if there are state or local laws you should know about that go above and beyond the federal requirements. Also, check www.bullypolice.org, where you can find details on harassment and bullying laws for each state.

4. What Are the Protected Classes of Students Covered Under These Laws?

There are legal consequences when harassment is based on race, color, religion, national origin, sex, gender stereotype, or disability. These are referred to as **protected classes**.

Keep in mind that harassment and bullying are harmful for all students, whether or not they are members of a legally protected class. We often hear insults that have to do with weight, height, clothing, hairdo, neighborhood, athletic coordination, and other characteristics that are not covered under federal, state, or local laws. But that doesn't mean these are any less damaging. You can use the STAND TALL tools with any type of harassment.

The OCR enforces laws that protect students against discrimination and harassment based on national origin, race, color, sex, and disability. The U.S. Department of Justice enforces laws that also protect students against harassment based on religion. In addition to these federal laws, check your state and local laws, which may specify additional protected classes, for example, based on sexual orientation, citizenship, and other characteristics. The website www.bullypolice .org keeps updated lists of protected classes for each state.

5. What Is a Hostile Environment?

When words or actions are sufficiently severe, persistent, or pervasive that they limit a student's ability to participate in or benefit from the education program—or when they create a hostile or abusive educational environment—this can constitute illegal harassment. The conduct must be unwelcome, a concept that can easily be misunderstood. Just because a student doesn't complain doesn't mean that the conduct was welcome. It may be that the student is afraid to speak up for fear of making matters worse.

Hostile environments take many forms. Here are some examples:

- name-calling
- making jokes and slurs that are ethnic, sexual, or racial in nature, based on gender stereotypes, religion, or disability
- telling lies or spreading rumors about a student's personal life or sexual life

- making comments about a student's anatomy or looks
- drawing or distributing cartoons, pictures, or graffiti that are racial, sexual, ethnic, religious, or based on gender stereotypes
- staring at someone in an intimidating or demeaning manner because of the person's race, color, or disability
- excluding a student from games, lunch tables, or other activities
- making fun of the way a student is dressed
- sending cruel email or text messages
- engaging in unwanted touching or physically blocking another student
- making threats
- making derogatory comments about a different religion, accent, or national origin

6. Which Carries More Weight: Intent or Impact?

In harassment cases, the standard is based on **impact.** It doesn't matter if a student says he or she was only joking around and didn't mean to offend anyone. School-based harassment does not have to include intent to harm, be directed at a specific target, or involve repeated incidents. Harassment creates a **hostile environment** "when the conduct is sufficiently severe, pervasive, or persistent so as to interfere with or limit a student's ability to participate in or benefit from the services, activities, or opportunities offered by a school" (OCR, 2010a).

This is a difficult concept to grasp, but the law has consistently found that harassment is in the eye of the beholder. Even if no harm was intended, when the result—the impact—creates a hostile environment, this can constitute illegal harassment. A hostile environment impacts not only the targeted student, but also other students who observe and are hurt, offended, humiliated, and upset. A hostile environment can have a negative impact on the attendance, attention, participation, and academic performance of all students.

7. What About Preventive Measures?

- Focus on respect. Talk about it, define it, reinforce it, model it, and praise others when you see it. Use STAND TALL to teach positive behaviors so that all students feel respected.
- Train everyone in the school community—all teachers, bus drivers, administrators, custodians, lunchroom and playground attendants—on the importance of respect, what types of disrespectful conduct can constitute harassment, and how to respond when they see it.

- Communicate and enforce a strong and clearly worded policy prohibiting harassment and bullying. Make sure that parents and students know about the policy, including information about grievance procedures and who to contact for information and help if they need it.

8. What Does "Know or Should Have Known" Mean?

I've seen more folks struggle with those five words! "How am I supposed to know what is going on with 35 different people at all times?" "Who's to say I should have known even though no one complained?" Here's how the OCR (2010a) explains **know or should have known**:

> In some situations, harassment may be in plain sight, widespread, or well-known to students and staff, such as harassment occurring in hallways, during academic or physical education classes, during extracurricular activities, at recess, on a school bus, or through graffiti in public areas. In these cases, the obvious signs of the harassment are sufficient to put the school on notice. In other situations, the school may become aware of misconduct, triggering an investigation that could lead to the discovery of additional incidents that, taken together, may constitute a hostile environment.

Bottom line: keep your antenna up. "I didn't see it happen" is not an excuse for failing to take appropriate action.

9. What Is Meant by "Prompt Corrective Action" in Response to Incidents of Harassment?

The OCR (2010a) says that the steps

> will vary depending upon the nature of the allegations, the source of the complaint, the age of the student or students involved, the size and administrative structure of the school, and other factors. In all cases, however, the inquiry should be prompt, thorough, and impartial.

If an investigation shows that harassment has occurred, the OCR recommends many different corrective actions, depending on the specific situation. Here are some examples from recently published guidelines (OCR, 2010b):

- separating the accused harasser and the target (minimizing the burden on the target)
- providing counseling for the target and/or the accused harasser
- taking disciplinary action against the harasser
- providing training, not only for the perpetrators, but also for the larger school community, to ensure that all students, their families, and school staff can recognize harassment if it recurs and know how to respond
- making sure that harassed students and their families understand the process and know how to report problems
- conducting follow-up inquiries to see if there have been any new incidents or incidents of retaliation
- responding promptly to address continuing or new problems
- hosting class discussions about racial harassment and sensitivity to students of other races
- conducting outreach to involve parents and students in ongoing efforts to identify problems and improve the school climate
- providing teachers with training to recognize and address anti-Semitic incidents
- providing training for staff in how to recognize and effectively respond to harassment of students with disabilities and monitoring to ensure that the harassment does not resume
- training students and employees on the school's policies related to harassment
- instituting new procedures by which employees should report allegations of harassment
- distributing contact information for the district's Title IX coordinator
- educating the entire school community on civil rights and expectations of tolerance, specifically as they apply to gender stereotypes

Your school policy may spell out additional requirements for prompt, corrective action, particularly with regard to speed and documentation.

10. What Should I Know About Our School Policy?

School policies vary, so be sure to read yours carefully. There should be a statement of purpose and scope; definitions of key terms like *harassment, bullying, cyberbullying, and retaliation;* and a description of procedures for reporting, documenting, and investigating complaints.

One aspect of the policy to look for is a description of the multiple channels for complaint. Harassment policies typically include several options for reporting a complaint. This is important. Generally speaking, students and parents can report harassment to the student's teacher, the principal, any school administrator, a counselor, or **another teacher**. You may find that students from other teachers' classes feel more comfortable talking to you if they have a problem. Listen to their whole story, then talk to your principal about the appropriate way to move forward.

Be clear about the policy requirement for confidentiality. The goal will be to investigate all incidents of harassment and take appropriate action, without violating due process and privacy rights. This gets complicated because of the Family Educational Rights and Privacy Act, so you definitely want to discuss this with your principal to decide the best way to handle a specific situation.

These policies and your legal responsibility are both critical and complicated. Remember that ignorance of the law is no excuse, so do all you can to stay current and focus on prevention. Creating and maintaining a positive, respectful learning community is your best hedge against legal problems.

3

Let's Talk About RESPECT for Individual Differences

STAND TALL teaches three core competencies:

These three competencies build on one another. Respect is the foundation.

Competency #1 Is RESPECT for Individual Differences

You can have a transformative effect on your students' academic achievement as well as social and emotional strength by teaching this competency. Use STAND TALL Module #1 to establish *respect* as the core of a positive learning environment. Then watch what happens.

I've seen amazing results in schools that make an ongoing commitment to teach students about respect. Come visit one of my favorites. It's in an industrial area, surrounded by auto body shops and taverns. Graffiti marks gang loyalties. A patchwork campus serves 516 elementary school students, many in prefab trailer classrooms. Ninety-five percent of the students are eligible for subsidized breakfast and lunch at school. My friend Marie, the school counselor, says the majority of students were considered "pre-gang" when she started working there. Yet their academic achievements are impressive, and *respect* is at the *core* of everything they do.

Walk into any classroom at this school, any morning, and listen in as the students and teachers recite first the Pledge of Allegiance and then the following "Pledge for Success."

Pledge for Success: A Promise I Make to Myself

I will listen to what others have to say.

I will treat others the way I would like to be treated.

I will **respect** the diversity of all people.

I will remember that I have people who care about me in my family, school, and community.

I will try my best.

A different student, using a pointer, leads the class through this pledge every day. The best part comes after the pledge is recited. The kids and teachers spend 3 minutes sharing examples of how the pledge came to mind the day before. Kids learn from each other what it means to respect themselves and others, and to deal with challenges, whether in the classroom or outside. They share examples like these: "When we were at the mall and I borrowed someone's cell phone to call 911 because my father was drunk and I was scared for him to drive. I remembered the promise to myself." "I remembered to respect myself and try my best when I still had a lot of homework but wanted to watch TV instead of doing it last night."

The daily Pledge for Success is one of the key actions this school has adopted as part of a whole-school commitment to create a positive culture and focus on respect. Another great tool to promote respect is their colorful "What I'm Proud Of" boards. Walk into any classroom for a fascinating portrait of the personal things kids list under their photos, and you'll see the rich tapestry that gives them strength and pride.

Since beginning this transformation, the school has measured significant achievement test score improvements: 33% in language arts and 44% in math.

> At another school that emphasizes respect as a core value, the director of education is certain that "just 10 minutes a day talking about respect saves hours every week of kids not paying attention and not learning."

Respect for individual differences is becoming much more critical all the time. We're in the midst of a major demographic shift with an ever-increasing mix of national origin, race, and religion across the country. What does this mean in your classroom? You probably already have a diverse group of students. The variety of national origins and family backgrounds can provide wonderful learning opportunities for lessons in geography, culture, history, arts, and language. Students can interview parents, grandparents, and extended family to prepare reports on countries and continents of origin and family traditions.

Be sure to review Chapter 7 for a range of curriculum-linked tools you can use to weave lessons about respect into language arts, social studies, math, art, physical education, and health. We've also included a fun and easy lesson plan, "Ancestor Detectives," at the end of this chapter. The time you devote to educating kids about respect will pay off. Watch for these results in your classroom:

- better classroom behavior and attention, making it easier to focus on schoolwork
- an appreciation of differences as a source of pride and honor, or, in kidspeak, making a paradigm shift away from "that's weird" to a new view: "that's cool"

- an expanded comfort zone so that kids can more successfully interact with different kinds of people at school . . . and throughout life

Here's how *you* start the process:

Introduce STAND TALL Video Episode #1

Tell the class they're going to be watching, then discussing, an exciting new program called STAND TALL. The program is about respect for differences—and how to handle situations when students are not respected or when they see someone else disrespected. You can tell them this is the first of three video episodes and your plan is to show one per week so they can talk about and learn from each episode. They will see a teacher named Jen (or, if you prefer, Ms. Hoyt) leading STAND TALL workshops with kids from six different schools. After the video, they'll have a chance to do some of the same exercises in class.

Establish Ground Rules

Tell the class it's important to think about what they need to have a good, safe discussion in which everyone feels comfortable participating. Because you will be talking about differences, some kids may have questions or ideas that others may not understand. That's why it helps to agree on a few ground rules in advance of the discussion. Here are a few you can suggest. Point out the acronym of PLUS, and ask your students what else they need to have a positive discussion:

- Participate by sharing your ideas and asking questions.
- Listen to others and talk one at a time.
- Use "I" messages.
- Say "Ouch" if someone says something that bothers you so we can learn from it.

Many of the best, most teachable moments I've witnessed were when someone said "Ouch" in response to an offensive comment. *Ouch* is an opportunity to pause and learn, then set a more positive climate. If you hear a comment that is disrespectful, be one of the first to say "Ouch." Say it loud and clear, even if a student who might be hurt won't speak up to do so. Take a moment to explain why you said it and move on. Your students will look to you to see what's acceptable and how to speak up when a comment or behavior is disrespectful. Use those moments to reinforce the skills of standing tall, speaking up in a way that is constructive, and sticking up for others.

Show . . . Then Discuss Video Episode #1

After the video, ask the class to work in small groups for the next 5 minutes to discuss these questions:

1. What did you like in the examples with the kids in the video? Which story was your favorite? Why?

2. How does it feel when you are treated with respect?

3. What actions and behaviors show that someone is being treated with respect?

After the small-group activity, share some of the good ideas with the class as a whole for the next 5 to 10 minutes. As you lead this discussion, you might refer to some of the following quotes from the video and ask your students if they agree/disagree/have different ideas about them:

Quote A: "Excluding other people can be disrespectful."

Quote B: "Interacting with everyone is a way to show respect."

Quote C: "The way you can show others that you're not judging them by their cover is to treat them with respect."

Exercise: I Am Someone Who . . .

Now use the exercise your students just watched in the video. Here's a suggested introduction (better in your own words):

So you can see from our discussion that there are many different ideas and experiences just in our class. Our differences can make things complicated, but they can also give us a lot to be proud of. Knowing more about each other's strengths and differences will make us stronger as a group and more successful as individuals. Let's play the game we just saw in the video to learn more about some of our differences.

Have your students stand in a line with room to move forward about 3 feet. Starting with the first child, have them take a step forward and complete the sentence "I am someone who. . . ." Anyone in the line who that statement also applies to should step forward. Continue down the line, asking them to try to come up with something that is unique to only them. If no one else can step forward, it means that the statement is truly unique, in which case the whole group cheers. Keep going until each child finds something unique about him- or herself and gets cheered.

This exercise is a powerful way to build respect for individual differences and self-esteem so that your students will stand taller. Charles Lee, PhD, a Cleveland-based educator and diversity consultant, shared a personal example with me:

> I remember as a child being initially concerned that I was being described as "four eyes." And I realized that they were talking about my eye glasses and my eyes. And I thought, "That's not how I see myself."
>
> So it was when I began to realize that I was a person who wore glasses as opposed to a person with four eyes, it made it much more difficult for people to hurt me. I think that's true of anybody who describes themselves as different and unique. If they accept the definition and attach esteem to it, they make themselves capable of standing tall.

Summarize Key Learning Points

Summarize STAND TALL Module #1 by asking your students what they learned about respect for individual differences. Record their ideas on the board. Be sure to emphasize these four learning points:

KEY LEARNING POINTS

1. There are lots of ways in which we're similar, and yet every one of us has qualities that make us unique.

2. Differences are not right or wrong; they're just different.

3. The things that make us different can be a source of pride, honor, and strength.

4. Everyone deserves to be treated with respect.

Follow-Up Ideas

Look for opportunities to reinforce these messages throughout the days that follow the video presentation and discussion. For example, take the time to acknowledge a student who responds to another student respectfully in a tense situation or takes the time to listen to what another student has to say. If you see a conflict based on differing skill levels, point out that skills vary and that the person who isn't good at one thing may be very good at something else. Explore that.

You can also choose a book from the list in Chapter 7 to read and discuss with your students. Choose a book about a child with a different cultural background from most of the children in your class.

You can use the following lesson plan as a follow-up exercise, if you'd like. Or maybe it will inspire you to create an exercise of your own. A homework assignment is included to enable family members and other people outside of the classroom to participate.

STAND TALL Lesson Plan
Ancestor Detectives

Focus: Classroom diversity

Grade Level: Grades 4–6

Subject Areas: History, geography, mathematics

Time: 10-minute homework explanation, 1-hour classroom activities

Materials:

- chart paper pinned to bulletin board
- markers
- sticker dots
- large map of the world
- map pins (one per country represented)

Overview:

Students interview their parents, grandparents, and other family members to find out which continents or countries their ancestors came from. Then students make a list. Their lists are anonymous. For Native American and African American ancestry, the family might not know the specific tribe or country of their ancestors, so continent of origin is enough. If the family knows specific countries, they can also provide that information.

Make up a chart from the lists that the kids turn in. Use sticker dots to record each time that country and continent occurs in a list. For example, if 10 students list Africa, there will be 10 sticker dots in the Africa row of the chart.

When the chart is complete, the class identifies the most common continents and countries of origin and the most unusual. The class helps to compute the fractional proportion and percentage of each nationality represented.

Look at the chart, and ask students to help you find each continent and country listed in the chart on a large map. Use pins to mark the continents or counties on the map. Have students note the geographical diversity of the class.

Objectives:

The primary objective of this lesson is to recognize that classrooms and individual students are usually blends of multiple cultural backgrounds.

- Student will learn more about their own family history.
- Students will recognize the cultural diversity within their own families.
- Students will engage in dialogue with family members.
- Students will show interest in other cultures.
- Students will share pride in their cultural traditions.

Introduction:

Define *ancestor* (parents, grandparents, parents of grandparents, etc.). Explain that many of our ancestors came to the United States from other countries, such as India, and that some students have Native American ancestors or ancestors from another continent, such as Africa. Tell students that their homework assignment is to do some detecting to find out the countries or continents their ancestors came from. Suggest that they talk to their parents and grandparents, if possible, to make up their list. They should also list the country where they were born. Have students ask their family partners to share a family story, favorite food, or tradition. Ask students to write down the story or a description of the food or tradition.

Procedure:

1. Hand out homework sheets a few days before the classroom exercise.

2. Number each list in the order you receive them, so they remain distinct but anonymous.

3. Make a chart with list numbers across the top row, and list all continents and countries represented in the first vertical column. Identify the countries listed within each continent as a subheading listed under that continent.

4. Pass the lists out randomly to students. Have each student read the countries or continents on the list they have been given while you place the dots in the appropriate columns.

5. The student can also read the family story, favorite food, or tradition reported on the homework sheet.

6. When the chart is complete, total up the number of dots in each country and continent row.

7. Have students help you figure out the proportion of the class with ancestors from each country and continent shown (total for each row over the total number of students in the class).

8. Ask students to help you convert the proportion to percentages.

9. Move to the wall map. Ask students to read the list of countries (or continents) and help you find each area to mark with a map pin (one pin per country).

10. Ask students if they are surprised to see how many countries are represented.

You can use the following homework form, based on the National Network of Partnership Schools' TIPS (Teachers Involve Parents in Schoolwork) interactive homework model.

Student Name: _____ Date: _____

Homework: Ancestor Detectives

Dear Family Partner:

    Each student in our class is asking our family partners to help us find out what continents and countries our ancestors came from. We are learning to appreciate our family heritage and individual identities. I can list any country or continent where my ancestors lived. I will also list the country where I was born. When I finish the list, I'd like you to choose and describe your favorite story, tradition, or food from one of those countries.

Here is an activity you can do with me. This assignment is due: _____

                    Sincerely, _____

                           (Student's signature)

Objective: To work together to find out where your ancestors lived and learn more about your cultural history.

Materials: Paper for a list of continents, countries, and description of your family partner's favorite family story, food, or tradition.

Procedure:

1. Ask your family partner to help you list the countries or continents where your ancestors have lived. You can ask other family members, such as grandparents, for help.

2. Make a list to take to school. You do not need to put your name on this list. Include the country where you were born.

3. When the list is done, ask your family partner to tell you a family story or describe a favorite family food or tradition.

4. Write the story or tradition on the same sheet as your list of countries or continents.

Conclusions:

1. Did either or both of you learn more about your family history?

2. Were you surprised at the number of countries you could list?

3. Had you heard this family story, participated in the family tradition, or eaten the food in the past?

_____

Home-to-School Communication

Dear Family Partner,

Please give me your reactions to your child's work on this activity. Write YES or NO for each statement.

_____ My child understood the homework and was able to discuss it.

_____ My child and I enjoyed the activity.

_____ This assignment helped me know what my child is learning in class.

Any other comments: _____

_____

Parent's signature: _____

4

Let's Have a Constructive DISCUSSION

I can hear Rod Stewart singing "I Don't Want to Talk About It" as I stare at this *New Yorker* cartoon:

"I have two mommies. I know where the apostrophe goes."

A lot of people *don't* want to talk about sexual orientation, race, ethnicity, family make-up, and other complicated topics. That's why I love the little boy in this cartoon. He knows what's up and he's happy to talk about it. *You* play a key role in the discussion.

Competency #2 Is DISCUSSION to Further Understanding

Kids notice everything. As Ronald Mah (2009), in *Getting Beyond Bullying and Exclusion,* says, "Pretending everyone is the same disrespects the uniqueness of individuals." In a conversation with me, he went on to say:

> Kids may hear their parents or other adults say they're color-blind or that race doesn't matter, but they don't buy it. Teachers can make respect and appreciation of differences integral parts of the classroom culture, leading to positive learning environments and higher levels of academic achievement.

You have to be able to talk honestly, age-appropriately, and respectfully, sometimes outside of your personal comfort zone. And you can build this skill in your students. You can teach them how to have constructive, respectful discussions about differences, and how to resolve conflicts peacefully.

Dean Jane Conoley, of the University of California Santa Barbara Gevirtz Graduate School of Education, points out that learning how to have a constructive discussion is a 21st-century skill that is "critical to learning how to think about problems, how to seek information and how to work with others to solve problems." In an interview I conducted with Dean Conoley, she added:

> Discussion and group work is also a great match with current standards, on both a content level and a process level. At the process level, the standards call for students to be able to seek information, to listen carefully, and to integrate information from a number of sources. On the content level, in social studies, health, and language arts, we expect students to know that people in the United States come to the classroom with different religions, different life experiences, and different ethnic customs. And it's only through discussion that children actually know that's true . . . that there's real difference in the foods I like, or the church or mosque or synagogue I go to, or

whether I have two moms, or two dads, or a mom and a dad of different genders.

Learning how to have constructive dialogue requires putting kids at the center of the discussion, giving them guidelines, feedback, and supervision. Learning how to have a constructive discussion includes learning conflict resolution. It's complicated. It's critical.

Let's take a quick peek into a classroom at another one of my favorite elementary schools, this one in a neighborhood with gorgeous trees and blooming vegetable gardens. The school's philosophy is based on three pillars: arts, academics, and relationships. A major component of the relationship pillar is teaching conflict resolution at all grade levels.

Just walk into Sonia's kindergarten classroom. Yes, I said kindergarten. Sonia invited me in when a student's grandmother put on an anti-bullying puppet show called "Hands Are NOT for Hitting." The kids liked the puppets, but the lesson itself didn't spark any lightbulbs. As one little boy stated after the show, "Kids at our school use our words, not our hands. We know conflict resolution." I almost fell out of my 16-inch-tall chair. Not missing a beat, though, Sonia built on this comment by asking the class to explain the steps in conflict resolution. Lots of hands shot up and I heard the children enthusiastically explain these steps:

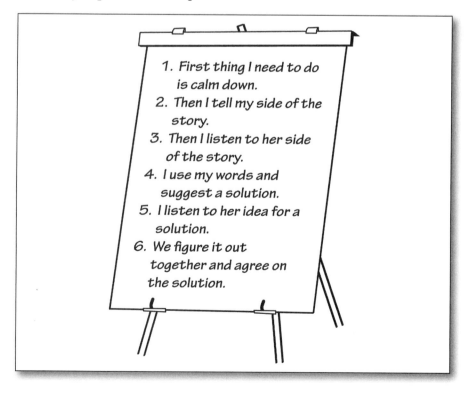

1. First thing I need to do is calm down.
2. Then I tell my side of the story.
3. Then I listen to her side of the story.
4. I use my words and suggest a solution.
5. I listen to her idea for a solution.
6. We figure it out together and agree on the solution.

Sonia praised the kids and reminded them that when they need help they can always go to a teacher, parent, sister, or brother. Fifteen minutes later I got to see the process in action when a conflict erupted. First a hurtful comment, then, "I didn't say that. You're a liar!" then red faces, then tearfully telling Sonia, "We need help with this conflict." It took Sonia exactly 3 minutes to work them through the process. Amazing. I just want you to know what's possible when kids learn how to have respectful discussions—even in kindergarten.

Chapter 7 includes tools and resources to teach your students how to have constructive discussions. Be sure to check out Ronald Mah's (2007) "Working It Out" downloadable lesson plan for a process that's easy for you to teach and for kids to use. Review the PLUS discussion guidelines, which are included in all three video episodes, to reinforce the learning outcomes for this module.

Introduce STAND TALL Video Episode #2

Tell the class that this is the second episode of the STAND TALL videos, and that it builds on the idea of respect that they talked about with the first episode. Describe a recent example of one of them showing respect and why that was good. With respect as the foundation, they will now learn how to have discussions that are constructive. They will see Jen, the same teacher from the first video, working with a different group of kids, showing them how to have a discussion that is constructive—especially when it's hard to do so. Take a minute to discuss the meaning of *constructive*.

Show . . . Then Discuss Video Episode #2

After the video, ask the class to work in small groups for the next 5 minutes to discuss these two questions:

1. What are words you can use to start off a constructive discussion?

2. In addition to "Ouch," what words can you use if you feel disrespected or hurt by someone's words or actions?

After the small-group activity, share some of the good ideas with the class as a whole for the next 5 to 10 minutes. As you lead this discussion, create two lists on the board: PLUS and OUCH. Under PLUS, record their words for having a constructive discussion. Also, refer to the PLUS ground rules posted earlier and add additional points if needed. Under OUCH, list their ideas for constructive ways to speak up if disrespected.

Exercise: What Can You Do?

Now, back in the small groups, have students pick one of the following three scenarios to discuss. Their task is to decide how to handle this type of situation. Encourage them to use strategies from the OUCH list you just created as well as new ideas.

1. "Someone at school makes jokes about my name. What should I do?"

2. "A boy at school said I was fat. What should I say to him when he says that kind of thing?"

3. Create their own scenario of a difficult conversation and figure out how to STAND TALL.

After 3 to 5 minutes, ask each group to share their example. Ask if some of them would like to role-play the situation in front of the class. As students describe how they would respond in these situations, emphasize that there are almost always several different choices for how to respond if disrespected, put down, teased, or insulted—or if they see this happen to someone else. Encourage your kids to brainstorm several different options, of course always including the following:

- telling the person you don't like what they said or did, and why you don't like it
- asking a friend to help out
- walking away
- talking with a teacher, parent, or other trusted adult

Summarize Key Learning Points

Summarize STAND TALL Module #2 by asking students what they learned. Record their ideas on the board, and emphasize these learning points:

KEY LEARNING POINTS

1. Sometimes it feels like you're tied up in knots, but it helps to talk about it.

2. Talking things out works when you treat everyone with respect.

3. There are ways to speak up when you feel disrespected that can make things better.

Keep It Alive

Set aside a regular classroom time for discussion of a story involving conflict resolution. It could be part of a social studies or language arts assignment, or it could reflect something that has happened in the classroom. Talk about how having a constructive discussion was key to successful resolution. Reinforce this module during the week with the following lesson plan, as well as other tools described in Chapter 7.

A homework assignment is included with the following lesson plan to allow family members and other people outside of the classroom to participate.

STAND TALL Lesson Plan
The Apology Tree

Focus: Name calling and other "ouch" words

Grade Level: Grades 4–6

Subject Areas: Language arts, life skills, health

Time: 30 to 40 minutes; 20 minutes follow up

Materials:

- small folded note card for each student
- hole punch
- strings
- tree with branches for hanging the cards

Overview:

Sticks and stones may break your bones, but words can really hurt! Identifying words and labels that are sometimes used thoughtlessly helps to increase awareness of the hurtful nature of these labels. *Sissy, wimp, gay, bitch, ugly, fat, stupid,* and *retard* are just a few examples.

Objectives:

- Student will recognize words that can be hurtful when talking about other students.
- Student will speak up when disrespectful language is used by another student.
- Student will apologize to other students when they realize they have hurt them.

Introduction:

Have the children sit on the floor in a circle, with their feet meeting in the center of the circle like the spokes of a wheel. You and any classroom assistants can join the circle.

Explain to the children that even words that are not bad words can be hurtful when said in a nasty way. Sometimes we use words to make other people feel bad on purpose. Sometimes we do it without realizing it might make the person we are talking to feel bad. Explain that these are "Ouch" words because they hurt, even if they were not meant to hurt.

Procedure:

1. Ask the children to think about a name or words that made them feel bad in the past, including when someone was just joking.

2. Start with yourself, then go around the circle and ask each child to share a name-calling word or words that made them feel bad.

3. When the circle comes back to you, explain why the name you were called hurt your feelings.

4. Ask the children to discuss different ways to tell someone that those words made them feel bad even if the person was joking.

5. Ask them to suggest ways to apologize to another person if you realize you have hurt them, whether you were mad at them or you didn't mean to hurt them. Talk about how apologies help to heal those bad feelings.

6. Give each child a card, and ask students to return to their desks.

7. Ask them to write down a word or words that made someone else feel bad on the front of the card, then, on the inside, write how they would apologize if they had said those words. Encourage them to think creatively about ways to say they're sorry.

8. String the cards and hang them onto an Apology Tree.

Follow-Up:

Have the children ask their parents (or other adults) if they remember being called a particularly hurtful name when they were kids, if they remember how it made them feel, and what they would say to that person if they could talk about it with them today. The next day, ask the children to share what they learned from their parents. Students can make cards with their parents' words and an apology to hang on the Apology Tree.

You can use the following homework form, based on the National Network of Partnership Schools' TIPS (Teachers Involve Parents in Schoolwork) interactive homework model.

Student Name: _____ Date: _____

Homework: Apology Tree

Dear Family Partner:

We've been learning about name calling and how to apologize when we use words that make other people feel bad. Sometimes we hurt someone on purpose because we are angry, and sometimes we do it accidentally. We are asking other people to share their past experiences with name-calling so that we can create an Apology Tree. Our class will hang note cards that share ideas about ways to apologize.

Here is an activity you can do with me. This assignment is due:

_____

Sincerely, _____

(Student's signature)

Objective: To think about how the words we use affect other people, sometimes hurting them and sometimes making them feel good.

Materials: Folded blank note cards (a 3″ × 5″ index card will work).

Procedure:

1. Ask your family partners about things that were said to them or names they were called when they were kids.

2. For each experience discussed, on the front of a folded note card, write the word or words that were used that made them feel bad.

3. Ask your family partners to explain what they would say to that person today if they talked about the incident with them and how that person could apologize. Write the apology on the inside of the note card. Don't be afraid to think of some fun ways to apologize.

4. You can make a card for each story you are told. Then bring them to school to hang on the Apology Tree.

Conclusions:

1. Were you surprised to hear about your family partner's experiences?

2. Does your family partner still feel a little sad about this experience?

3. Did you think of some new ways to apologize?

Home-to-School Communication

Dear Family Partner,

Please give me your reactions to your child's work on this activity. Write YES or NO for each statement.

_____ My child understood the homework and was able to discuss it.

_____ My child and I enjoyed the activity.

_____ This assignment helped me know what my child is learning in class.

Any other comments: _____

_____

Parent's signature: _____

5

Let's Talk About
ACTION and Options

Now that your students have learned a lot about Respect and Discussion, let's build the third STAND TALL competency: ACTION.

Some of the hardest, saddest stories told by kids who've been bullied are those in which the child felt totally helpless. Even worse, of course, are those that resulted in death.

There are two strikingly similar photos over my desk. One is Tyler Clementi, on the cover of *People* magazine (headline: DEADLY BULLYING). Next to it is a picture of my older son, Doug. It almost could be the same kid . . . same coloring, glasses, nose, shape of face, cute little grin. Both smart kids and talented musicians. Doug, 10 years older than Tyler, is enjoying a fabulous career as a music director and married his partner in June. Why did Tyler Clementi have to miss all of this by being driven to suicide simply because of difference?

Kids need to know that there are constructive actions and options to consider when things are rough. Despite your best efforts, there will still be insults, teasing, name-calling, and behaviors that are hurtful. And your students should *not* feel helpless. They need to know that they have safe and constructive options—actions they can take and people who can help.

Walk out onto the sun-baked dirt playground with me at another favorite school. It's lunchtime, so dozens of kids are running around, eating and playing—the typical hectic, noisy scene. But look a little closer and you'll see two kids wearing red capes. They are today's designated Peace Makers.

Wendy and the Peace Makers is not a 1960s rock band. Wendy is the teacher who trains every fifth-grade student in this school to be a Peace Maker. The children participate in six 45-minute classes, spread out over 3 weeks, then have the option of taking on the role for a designated recess or lunch period. There are two Peace Makers per period, and it's not hard to fill the weekly schedule. Here's what some of the kids in red capes told me:

"It feels good to help people get their problems solved."

"You learn how to deal with problems in the future."

"You feel strong when you stick up for someone."

Sticking up for others is one of the key learning points in this module. You can teach your students how to be *upstanders* rather than bystanders when they observe bullying, harassment, or disrespectful behavior. As Walter Roberts, author of *Bullying From Both Sides*, states in the STAND TALL video:

We can't follow kids around, and it's not our job to solve all their problems. When we teach them to be an upstander rather than a bystander, we give them the behavioral tools to be able to go up to another individual and be assertive, not aggressive, and say "Hey, that's not appropriate. Don't do that." When kids do it in their own world, it's ten times more powerful than anything that we'll ever be able to do as an adult.

Introduce STAND TALL Video Episode #3

Tell the class that this is the third episode of STAND TALL and it builds on all they've been learning about RESPECT and DISCUSSION. Describe a recent example of a constructive discussion in which your students resolved a conflict, came to a new understanding, and/or created something they're proud of. The third module will build on all of that and focus on ACTION. Students will see that there are many ways to respond in a tough situation. They always have options. They can make smart choices. And they will learn the difference between being a bystander and being an upstander.

Show . . . Then Discuss Video Episode #3

After the video, ask the class to work in small groups for the next 5 to 10 minutes to discuss the following:

1. What words and actions did the kids in the video suggest for how to respond in disrespectful situations? List as many as they remember, not just the comment "Dude, don't do that."

2. What other actions/options might work when they see or experience disrespect? Add those ideas to the list.

Bring the whole class back together. Write SMART CHOICES on the board or a flip chart.

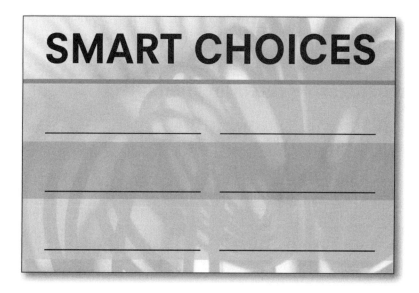

Go round-robin to have each small group suggest one of the options from their list. As each idea is shared, ask the class if they think that's an option that would work for them. Why or why not? Facilitate a 10-minute discussion to have your kids articulate why each option can help them STAND TALL . . . or not. Record their SMART CHOICES on the flip chart.

Exercise: The Mojo Game

Back in their small groups, ask students to interview each other, with this request:

> Tell me a story about a time when you stood up for someone or when someone stood up for you.

Advise the kids to include as many details of the story as possible. After 2 or 3 minutes, tell students to swap roles and take enough time for each child to share a story. Then ask the small groups to pick one of their favorite stories to share with the whole class. They may either role-play the scenario in front of the class or simply tell the story that one of them shared in the small group. Tell the class to listen for the power involved when someone acts as an upstander and call out **"Mojo"** when they hear it. Facilitate discussion of these questions:

- How does it feel when you stand up for another person who is being disrespected?
- How does it feel to have someone stand up for you?
- What's the difference between being a bystander and being an upstander? Why do you think it's good to be an upstander?

Summarize Key Learning Points

Summarize STAND TALL Module #3 by asking students what they learned. Record their ideas on the board and emphasize these learning points:

KEY LEARNING POINTS
1. Stand up for yourself and your friends when you experience or observe disrespect—be an upstander, not a bystander.
2. Remember that you always have options, and make smart choices.
3. Use your mojo and be strong!

Keep It Alive

Here are some words of wisdom from Dean Jane Conoley:

> Intervene when you see a problem so that you can catch it low to prevent it from going high. When children are intervened with early, if they're starting to be disrespectful, harassing or bullying, the quicker we can intervene and let them know that this is not appropriate, the better.

Sometimes when you intervene, suggest that students role-play a better way to handle the situation. Charles Lee points out that

> role-playing and simulations are so valuable because students can stand outside of themselves and learn from it. And the wonderful thing is that they can walk away with some learning and tools to use in real life.

You can use the following lesson plan as a follow-up exercise, if you'd like. Or maybe it will inspire you to create an exercise of your own. A homework assignment is included to allow family members and other people outside of the classroom to participate.

STAND TALL Lesson Plan
STAND TALL Hero Awards

Focus: Inspiring stories of people who stand up to harassment, bullying, or disrespect

Grade Level: Grades 4–6

Subject Areas: Language arts, social studies, art, physical education, and health

Time: Introduction to homework: 10 minutes. Hero discussion, vote, and project planning: 30 minutes. Project development: 45 minutes. Presentation: 1 hour

Materials:

- folder for each group to compile stories from family, neighbors, and friends
- award certificates for each group
- art materials as needed for each group's project

Overview:

Students talk with family, neighbors, and friends about the decision to be an upstander and gather stories of someone who stood tall in response to a disrespectful situation. These can be stories of a personal experience, a historical event, or an inspiring story that someone has heard.

Divide the class into groups of four or five students. Each group discusses the stories they have collected and votes on the STAND TALL hero story they like best. Once they have identified their hero, students should discuss how the hero's actions helped to restore respect.

Students will choose a way to illustrate the actions of their STAND TALL hero. For example, they could create and act out a skit; write a newspaper article; give a radio report; create an art project, cartoon, storybook, or puppet show. At a gathering with parents and family present, each group will announce their STAND TALL Hero Award and give the presentation they created to illustrate the actions they are honoring.

Objectives:

To inspire students to look for examples of STAND TALL behavior and model that behavior.

- Students will identify actions that create an environment of respect.
- Students will share ideas and come to a consensus.
- Students will collaborate to create a presentation.
- Students will learn safe and healthy ways to respond to disrespect.
- Students will recognize that one person can make a difference.

Introduction:

Explain that conflict is a normal part of everyday life and that there are many ways to respond to conflict. Some ways are respectful, and some are not.

When we experience or see disrespectful behavior, we have the option to STAND TALL and speak up. This is not always easy, but it's very important for keeping our classroom, playground, and school community a safe and healthy place for all students.

Explain to students that the first part of this project will be to collect stories about people who chose to STAND TALL when they experienced or observed disrespect.

Procedure:

1. Ask students to interview family, neighbors, and friends for stories of someone who chose to STAND TALL in response to a disrespectful situation. Explain that this can be a personal experience, a historical event, or a story they have heard.

2. Pass out the homework sheets. Give students several days to gather their stories.

3. Divide the class into groups of four or five students. Give each group a folder to collect their stories.

4. When the stories are in, ask students to share and discuss the stories within their groups, then vote on the hero story they like the best.

5. Ask students to discuss the actions their chosen hero took to restore respect.

6. Have students fill out an award certificate for their chosen STAND TALL hero.

7. Explain that their families will be invited to a presentation to honor the STAND TALL heroes they have chosen.

8. Ask them to develop a short presentation that illustrates the actions of the hero they have chosen. They can create a skit, news report, art project, storybook, or cartoon depiction of the event.

9. Invite family and friends to attend the presentations.

Student Name: _____ Date: _____

Homework: STAND TALL Heroes

Dear Family Partner:

We are learning about ways to take action when we see or experience disrespect. For a classroom project, we need your help in gathering stories of people who chose to STAND TALL to stop bullying and harassment. These stories can be personal experiences, historical events, or inspiring stories you have heard. It can be about a hero as inspiring as Rosa Parks, or as simple as someone responding to a rude comment at a baseball game. This is an activity you can do with me. We can ask other people such as neighbors and friends about stories they have experienced or observed.

Our class will select hero stories to illustrate. We will honor our chosen STAND TALL heroes and share their stories in a classroom event. We hope that you will join us on _____ at _____ in _____ for our presentation.

This assignment is due: _____

Sincerely, _____

(Student's signature)

Objective:

To identify inspiring stories of people who chose to STAND TALL in the face of disrespect.

Materials:

Sheets of paper to record the stories. One sheet per story.

Procedure:

1. The student will discuss what it means to STAND TALL.

2. The family partner will help the student identify personal experiences or historical or remembered events where an individual chose to STAND TALL.

3. The student will write down the stories to take to class.

Conclusions:

1. Were you surprised at how many examples you could find of someone who chose to STAND TALL?

2. Did your family partner share a personal experience in which someone who chose to STAND TALL made a difference?

3. Do you feel inspired to be a STAND TALL hero?

Home-to-School Communication

Dear Family Partner,

Please give me your reactions to your child's work on this activity. Write YES or NO for each statement.

_____ My child understood the homework and was able to discuss it.

_____ My child and I enjoyed the activity.

_____ This assignment helped me know what my child is learning in class.

Any other comments: _____

_____

Parent's signature: _____

6

STAND TALL
With Your Community

Academic achievement and a strong community are both highly compatible and mutually interdependent. It is impossible for most students to achieve academically if they do not feel safe, supported, welcomed and accepted. A strong classroom community is the foundation on which all of our work must rest.

Mara Sapon-Shevin, *Because We Can Change the World*

The three core competencies of STAND TALL can be used to strengthen your school community and enhance academic achievement. This chapter suggests ideas, offers tools, and describes eight great examples of ways to reach out to parents and the larger community for mutual success.

RESPECT

Think about everyone in your larger community who shares this goal: to provide the best possible education for the children in your classroom and in your school. Parents, of course, lead the list, so let's start there. As President Obama (2008) said, "There is no program and no policy that can substitute for a parent who is involved in their child's education from day one."

Parents are a teacher's bridge to building community within a classroom, a school, and the larger community. Nancy Oster, developmental editor for this book, is also a chef. She describes how her involvement in the classroom seemed like a natural extension of her role as a parent and enriched her life as well.

> As a young parent, I welcomed the opportunity to spend time in the classroom helping the teacher with activities that enriched classroom curriculum. For example, when the class was studying the California gold rush, I made a sourdough starter with the kids and then we made sourdough pancakes. While working in the classroom I met the other students. When I helped on field trips and at special events I met their parents. The classroom and school were an important part of our family life.

Social and emotional skill development begins at home. Ideally, teachers and parents can work together to reinforce positive social and emotional lessons. Still, parents have very different needs, work schedules, priorities, communication preferences, and ways they can contribute. Not everyone can come to school like Nancy did to make pancakes with the class. So it's important to convey respect for parents with different perspectives, strengths, and schedules. Get to know them and find ways they can participate and contribute.

Respecting that not all parents have the time available to work in the classroom, Dr. Joyce Epstein, director of the Center on School, Family, and Community Partnerships and the National Network of Partnership Schools, has developed *Epstein's Framework of Six Types of Involvement* to help teachers find ways to encourage more parent and community participation. Dr. Epstein's work focuses on how to implement and support parent involvement. Figure 6.1 explains her six keys.

A detailed description of the framework and a bevy of tools to achieve these goals are available at www.csos.jhu.edu/p2000. Check it out. You're sure to find at least a couple of ideas that will support your goals.

DISCUSSION

Whose voices should be heard as you discuss this goal: to provide the best possible education for the children in your community. Who has a stake in the outcome? Parents, of course, but be sure to also think

Figure 6.1

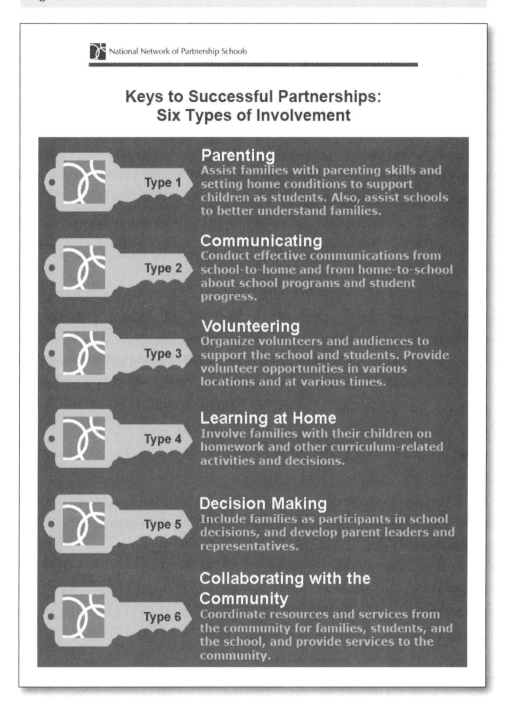

National Network of Partnership Schools

Keys to Successful Partnerships:
Six Types of Involvement

Type 1
Parenting
Assist families with parenting skills and setting home conditions to support children as students. Also, assist schools to better understand families.

Type 2
Communicating
Conduct effective communications from school-to-home and from home-to-school about school programs and student progress.

Type 3
Volunteering
Organize volunteers and audiences to support the school and students. Provide volunteer opportunities in various locations and at various times.

Type 4
Learning at Home
Involve families with their children on homework and other curriculum-related activities and decisions.

Type 5
Decision Making
Include families as participants in school decisions, and develop parent leaders and representatives.

Type 6
Collaborating with the Community
Coordinate resources and services from the community for families, students, and the school, and provide services to the community.

about the larger community. Who else comes to mind? Quickly list half a dozen community organizations, civic groups, local businesses, and people who also share this same goal.

1. _____

2. _____

3. _____

4. _____

5. _____

6. _____

Did your list include grandparents, local employers, government officials, social service organizations, law enforcement representatives, parks and recreation departments, community colleges, retiree groups, and philanthropic and faith-based groups?

This may seem like a daunting task. Just start the discussion with parents. They probably have relationships with many of these groups and know individuals who can open doors. Inclusion of the larger community can bring in new volunteer workers, increase financial support for your school, and expand educational opportunities for your students. And it all starts with discussion. Discussion leads to building relationships and developing shared goals. Read on for some best practices to help you start the discussion.

ACTION

This section presents **eight great strategies**, based on examples that cross the country, all with successful outcomes. Use what fits your school as you develop an action plan to build, strengthen, and leverage the resources of your community.

Communicate Proactively With Parents

The director of education at Santa Barbara Charter School (SBCS), Bev Abrams, sent the following letter to the parents of all students to engage them as partners in understanding and responding to harassment and bullying. She offers it as a template for other schools to use. Her rationale is that "15 minutes per day of talking about respect can save you hours per week of administrative time spent on discipline and parent communication that is reactive." This is a great example of parent communication that is *proactive.*

Dear Parents,

Recently there have been several high-profile incidents of bullying in the news. Many newspapers and magazines have run articles on the subject. Nearly everyone can remember the pain of being teased or harassed at some moment in their life, and we worry about our own children experiencing similar hurt and humiliation. Parents often choose SBCS because of our focus on communication and relationships, and therefore may feel quite distressed when becoming aware of conflicts and teasing in school. Given the visibility of this issue, it seems timely to review the way teachers and other adults respond to this kind of behavior at SBCS.

What is bullying?

Bullying usually refers to some form or other of intimidation. Intimidation may be an attempt to establish power physically or verbally. While the term *bullying* is used in common conversation, we avoid the term at SBCS.

Why don't we refer to "bullies" or "bullying" at SBCS?

The term *bully* is a label that doesn't identify problems or resolve conflicts. Just as we don't call children *tattletale* or *lazy,* we don't refer to them as *bullies* or their behavior as *bullying.* As a few of our fourth and fifth graders stated, "If we tell you that someone is bullying us, you don't know what they have done. . . . You don't know how to help us. . . . They might have hurt or teased us, but if we don't explain, you don't know." Our goal is to facilitate the students' ability to address interpersonal concerns in order to create a physically and emotionally safe environment. We encourage students to identify specific concerns such as name-calling, teasing, bad language, threats, gossip, insults, roughhousing, hitting, kicking, or pushing. Students are guided through the steps of conflict resolution. They learn to use "I-messages" as well as to empathize with the feelings of the other child(ren) so that meaningful resolution can be reached.

Why do children engage in these behaviors that hurt others?

There are both obvious and more subtle reasons for these kinds of behaviors. All people need to explore their own sense of personal power. Our task is to help children recognize this need and find ways to empower

(Continued)

(Continued)

them without causing harm to others. Sometimes students feel a heady sense of belonging when they join together to tease another. Developing a sense of empathy and exploring more positive ways to connect with others address this underlying dynamic. Sometimes children are misunderstood because they play hard on the soccer field, attempt to defend friends, or stand up for someone in a way that seems threatening. In these instances, helping children on both sides to talk through their feelings and reactions is essential.

As children become older, teasing or name-calling often begins as a mutually acceptable activity. However, students often don't understand that there is an invisible line that can be crossed, resulting in hurt feelings, anger, and even physical confrontation. Sometimes the student who initiates the teasing is the one who is most upset with the direction it takes. It takes time and care to reach resolution.

Recently a group of our students explained that you shouldn't engage in teasing, taunting, name-calling, or roughhousing "because others who see you might not know you, and they might think it is okay to join in when it's not." Moreover, students recognized that students who are teased sometimes come to internalize the names that they have been called. Additionally, students may feel generally unsafe when there is a climate of harsh banter. All agreed that it would be best if these behaviors didn't happen in school.

Why aren't children automatically punished when they do mean things?

Most research indicates that these behaviors are best addressed through education and communication. Students benefit from learning conflict resolution and problem-solving skills. Establishing policies that indicate potential consequences is important because such policies are an expression of the school's values and culture. However, we avoid "zero-tolerance" policies because they preclude potential conversations and understandings that grow out of more flexible responses. Punishment is really best saved for those rare occasions when behavior is repeated or widespread and needs to be suppressed immediately.

If staff at SBCS are serious about cultivating an emotionally and physically safe environment, why do teasing and aggressive behavior persist?

Part of growing up includes trying on all kinds of behavior. Children explore friendship and power in many different ways, and both will continue to be important elements in their lives as adults. Damage is done when there is tacit approval in a school for behavior that victimizes the underdog. However, real growth, awareness, and power come from meaningful communication and conflict resolution. Incidents that include taunting, threats, or even physical conflict are opportunities for cultivating these skills in real-life situations. Students leave SBCS better able to deal with these behaviors when they encounter them in other settings.

Aside from helping children to learn nonaggressive ways for engaging with others and empowering themselves, we believe that it is also important to teach them not to become victims. Some children learn that being a victim is a powerful way to gain attention. Rather than reinforcing this dynamic, we encourage students to find other ways to gain attention from adults and other children. An important rule in some classes is "Don't hurt others and don't let yourself get hurt." This guideline asks children to take responsibility for behavior that might prompt negative responses from others.

What can parents do when their children come home unhappy because someone has been mean to them?

1. Encourage your child to be specific.

2. There are usually at least two sides of a story, so try to get the whole picture. Ask questions such as: What happened first? What were you doing or saying before this happened?

3. Insist that your child let adults at school know when something upsetting happens in school. Problems can't be addressed when nobody knows about them. If your child is initially reluctant to share their concerns, accompany them to speak to their teacher. Let your child know that the goal is for them to learn to let the teachers know when things happen.

4. Recognize that most of us suffer when we think that our children are being hurt in ways that we remember from our own childhood. Try to separate your own feelings from the immediate situation. Help empower your child (possibly with situational strategies such as those found in *The King of the Playground,* by Phyllis Reynolds Naylor) so that they don't end up feeling like a victim.

5. Try asking, "Do you want me to do something about it, or did you just want me to know?" as a way to identify a child who needs to vent versus a problem that needs solving.

6. Let your child's teacher know any time that your child is coming home from school unhappy. It is important to uncover the source of such feelings. Often there will be things that the teachers and other staff members can do to make your child feel safer or more comfortable.

There are some great messages in Bev's letter to parents, especially the importance of not labeling kids and how to talk accurately about behavior. Feel free to adapt this letter or excerpts from it as part of your proactive communication with parents. It's best not to wait for an incident of bullying and harassment before getting this type of communication out to parents.

Another tool for proactive communication with parents about bullying and harassment is provided by the U.S. Department of Health and Human Services (n.d.). Parents who know that you care

Table 6.1 Warning Signs of Bullying and Harassment

Being Bullied

- Comes home with damaged or missing clothing or other belongings
- Reports losing items such as books, electronics, clothing, or jewelry
- Has unexplained injuries
- Complains frequently of headaches, stomachaches, or feeling sick
- Has trouble sleeping or has frequent bad dreams
- Has changes in eating habits
- Hurts themselves
- Is very hungry after school from not eating his lunch
- Runs away from home
- Loses interest in visiting or talking with friends
- Is afraid of going to school or other activities with peers
- Loses interest in schoolwork or begins to do poorly in school
- Appears sad, moody, angry, anxious, or depressed when she comes home
- Talks about suicide
- Feels helpless
- Often feels like he is not good enough
- Blames herself for her problems
- Suddenly has fewer friends
- Avoids certain places
- Acts differently than usual

Bullying Others

- Becomes violent with others
- Gets into physical or verbal fights with others
- Gets sent to the principal's office or detention a lot
- Has extra money or new belongings that cannot be explained
- Is quick to blame others
- Will not accept responsibility for his actions
- Has friends who bully others
- Needs to win or be best at everything

Source: Department of Health and Human Services (www.stopbullying.gov/topics/warning_signs).

about the safety and well-being of their children are more likely to participate in keeping the school climate healthy and fostering constructive communication. So consider sharing this list and encouraging parents to contact the school if they observe these warning signs.

Educate Your Community

We all should know that diversity makes for a rich tapestry, and we must understand that all threads of the tapestry are equal no matter what their color.

Maya Angelou, *Wouldn't Take Nothing for My Journey Now*

Tapestry Cards—University of Chicago Hospitals and Health System

Imagine that you work in a large university hospital located in an economically and ethnically diverse area. In a single day you might hear 20 different languages being spoken and meet people from all over the world while walking through the corridors. Overwhelming? Yes! That was what led the staff at University of Chicago Hospitals and Health System to create their award-winning Tapestry Cards program.

To help the medical staff be culturally competent, notebooks were placed at every nursing station throughout the hospital complex. Each notebook contained a collection of laminated Tapestry Cards. Each card identified the cultural characteristics and traditions of one of the nationalities the staff might encounter during a shift. The information included customs, holidays, a language glossary of words they might need in order to communicate with a patient or family member, and ways to show respect for various religious traditions. The "must know" information on the cards was contributed by diverse staff members and compiled by the hospitals' Diversity Committee.

In a multicultural school, teachers, administrators, and staff often need the same sort of information. For example, the meaning of gestures, marks of respect that might vary by age or gender, body language, and nonverbal communication all come into play when working with students and communicating with parents. A Tapestry Card project can be organized by the school PTA and compiled by the kids and parents, with teachers and administrators identifying the type of practical information they would find useful. Like the medical staff, school personnel need this basic understanding to be culturally competent and cultivate an environment of respect.

Develop Student Leaders

Team LEAD

To create behavioral change among children, they must take ownership of that change.

> Peggy Buffington, Superintendent of Schools,
> School City of Hobart, Indiana

How exactly is that done? By giving kids the opportunity to become leaders and supporting their work. Team LEAD is a leadership program that empowers student leaders with social knowledge, resilience, character, and communication skills. Older students from elementary, middle, and high school are trained to become mentors to the younger students in their schools. To become mentors, students must commit to the philosophy of Team LEAD and sign a contract honoring their commitment to support and actively promote positive social norms.

Team LEAD promotes **L**eadership, **E**mpathy, **A**ccountability, and open **D**iscussion.

Understanding that friends help and support each other with kind words and actions, students are empowered to take a leadership role in creating a more positive social climate for all members of the school community. Team members sign a contract agreeing on a daily basis to do the following:

1. Participate in CONSCIOUS acts of kindness regularly.

2. Starve the Flame of Aggression by giving it NO support.

3. Refrain from name-calling.

4. Show respect and consideration for peers and adults.

5. Avoid gossip and rumors; change the subject, do not pass it on.

6. Include others rather than excluding them.

7. Listen for put-downs and insults, and STOP them by saying something nice and refraining from laughing.

8. SUPPORT THE TARGET. The most helpful things kids can do for other kids involves just listening and being there for each other.

9. Watch how you treat your own circle of friends; in fact, this is the best place to start and sometimes the hardest place to change your behavior.

10. Be positive role models for all kids in the building and beyond. (Koebcke, 2010)

The elementary school leadership program is open to fourth and fifth graders who create service projects and mentor younger students. At the middle school level, students are mentored in leadership by Team LEADers from the local high school. In all cases, the older students model positive social behavior and become a catalyst for change with younger students in their school community.

> As one of the Team LEAD students said, "Team LEAD has kind of changed my life, because I am actually getting better grades now. I am helping other kids stop making wrong decisions and keeping more friends out of trouble."

Empower Students to Be Agents of Positive Change

Civil Rights Team Project, Office of the Attorney General, Maine

Sometimes the best ideas come from the students themselves. Present a problem, discuss it, and encourage students to come up with solutions. Empower them to channel some of that extra energy into leadership.

The State of Maine has been doing exactly that since 1996, when the state's Office of the Attorney General launched the Civil Rights Team Project (CRTP). This student-led program is designed to increase student safety by reducing bias and harassment in Maine's elementary, middle, and high schools. Today more than 180 schools have civil rights teams.

A team consists of any number of students who collaborate with at least one adult advisor to implement their ideas for raising student awareness and building a healthy, safe environment in their school as well as in the larger community. Students learn that what they do has an impact and that they can be agents of positive change.

Projects have ranged from posting positive messages on the bulletin boards throughout the school to organizing a Diversity Day that included multicultural performances, speakers from the larger community, discussions, and a video the students created for the school to view and use for future reflection and growth.

You can begin at the classroom level by encouraging students to identify ways to raise student and staff awareness and improve your school climate. Assemble the students into small teams to brainstorm. They might want to make a presentation to another class, plan a class project, or create ongoing teams like Maine's CRTP. See what they think!

Partner With Local Law Enforcement

G.R.E.A.T. (Gang Resistance Education and Training),
U.S. Department of Justice

Thanks to a U.S. Department of Justice program, you can enlist the help of your local police department as a proactive teaching resource. In an effort to prevent gang involvement in communities throughout the United States, the Bureau of Justice Assistance trains police officers throughout the country to teach classes in local elementary and middle schools.

The curriculum includes teaching life skills such as how to handle anger, how to recognize and respond to bullying, effective ways to communicate respectfully, and when to ask an adult for help. Police officers will come to your school to teach six 30- to 45-minute lessons and provide handouts for students to take home to share with their parents. The police officer's efforts can reinforce other prevention programs, such as STAND TALL, and help develop a positive relationship between kids and law enforcement officers.

To find out more about the program and what is available in your area, go to www.great-online.org.

Train Mentors

Project Change: You Have the Power!
Montgomery County, Maryland

At home, on the playground, and after school, younger kids are influenced by what they see older kids doing and hear them saying. On more than one occasion, you've probably had to step in to correct or mediate behaviors learned from older friends and siblings.

The good news is that older students can also inspire younger students in positive ways. In Montgomery County, Maryland, a group of community leaders works with local teens to identify and develop teen-led service projects that respond to local problems in their communities. Project Change was founded in 1998 by four high school students, joined by a group of adults who actively supported their creativity, problem solving, and leadership skills.

In 2004, a group of teenaged Project Change high school members proposed a mentoring program to reduce bullying in local middle and elementary schools. The You Have the Power! (YHTP!) Bullying Prevention Peer Education Project was created as a teen-taught after-school program to help younger kids learn how to respond to and prevent bullying in their schools. These teen teachers also collaborate with younger students on ways to use their personal power to strengthen and improve their school and community environments.

YHTP! has received national recognition as a model program and has published a YHTP! Toolkit, available at www.projectchange-md .org, to help teens in communities everywhere become mentors. The U.S. Department of Health and Human Services also offers a Youth Leaders' Toolkit (available at www.stopbullying.gov), based on the YHTP! Project, to empower teens in other communities to develop similar programs.

Develop a Pledge

A pledge sets the tone for a safe school environment and communicates expectations for how people will act within that environment. A pledge can be developed by a classroom or by a school committee. It reminds students and staff of the principles that guide their school community.

What's in a pledge? The It Gets Better Project has developed a pledge as a show of support for lesbian, gay, bisexual, and transgender (LGBT) youth. The pledge raises awareness, affirms support, creates buzz, and gathers momentum for the project. The It Gets Better Project has harnessed the power of the Internet to collect and publish thousands of stories of encouragement from LGBT adults and youth, as well as their friends, families, and famous folks such as Hillary Clinton and Ellen DeGeneres.

The It Gets Better Project pledge begins "Everyone deserves to be respected for who they are. I pledge to spread this message to my friends, family and neighbors. I'll speak up against hate and intolerance whenever I see it, at school and at work." This is a terrific beginning for any pledge dedicated to preventing bullying and harassment. But make it your own. Here are some general guidelines:

- Emphasize respect.
- Keep it positive.
- Focus on actions.
- Make it short, simple, and memorable.

Allow for all segments of the school population—including students and parents—to participate in drafting the pledge as well as work on ways to promote and use it. The PTA would be a valuable partner in this project. A pledge that is developed by your students and school community should be in their words and reflect their conviction.

For more information about the It Gets Better Project, go to www.itgetsbetter.org.

Tap Community Resources

AHA! Support for Teachers and Students

"Teachers often feel pressured to focus on the blackboard," says Academy of Healing Arts (AHA!) cofounder Jennifer Freed. "Teachers need to be able to focus on the emotional climate of the classroom, not just academic performance." But Jennifer and her founding partner, Rendy Freedman, realized that those teachers needed help to do so.

So they responded by forming AHA!, a nonprofit organization that offers in-school, afterschool, and summer programs for students in Santa Barbara, California, public schools. Both women are licensed family therapists, psychology professors, and trained mediators who work alongside local schools to help students build character, emotional intelligence, imagination, and social conscience. Using awareness games, dialogue, creative expression, and team-building exercises, they help students give voice to their inner feelings, find community among their peers, and begin to take leadership roles in their community.

The support of these two women helps teachers bridge the gap between academic instruction and social and emotional learning needs. Additionally, AHA! has been lauded for its anti-bullying techniques and emphasis on celebrating diversity. This inclusive approach has led to significant reductions in violent behavior and behavior-related suspensions on campuses where AHA! exists.

In this example, counseling professionals partnered with local middle schools and high schools to create a variety of programs. Outreach to skilled members of the community can provide resources that support schools and strengthen the larger community at the same time. Nonprofits and businesses are often eager to find ways to give back to their community and to support the next generation of leaders. Outreach to professionals, organizations, and businesses can provide unexpected resources and help build rapport between schools and the broader community. So just ask!

Keep It Alive

This chapter has eight examples of ways to STAND TALL with your community. Talk to parents and, of course, your students for additional ideas to make a difference. Review the programs, books, and resources that follow in Chapter 7. Consider sending out a quick survey to parents and others with just two questions to get feedback and new ideas as you use STAND TALL.

Whether your progress with STAND TALL shows early improvement in the three core competencies or you feel like it'll be an uphill journey lasting forever, you can have a tremendous impact in shaping skills that your students will use throughout their lives. My dear friend Judy Meisel, civil rights activist and Holocaust survivor, says it best: "One person can still make a difference, especially a teacher."

7

Compendium of Additional Resources

The Internet presents a continuously changing array of resources. A search on "bullying" will bring up an overwhelming number of results. For help getting started, we offer a quick reference list to get you to some of the primary information and resource sites. Don't forget to bookmark the sites you like, and always look to see if they offer lists of additional resource links.

We also list books you can read in the classroom as a supplement to the STAND TALL videos and exercises. There's more than enough to pick a book a week for the entire school year! Our book list also includes helpful books for teachers and parents.

Federal Agencies

U.S. Department of Education

www.ed.gov

Establishes policies, collects data, oversees research, directs attention to major issues in education, and enforces laws prohibiting harassment and discrimination in federally funded programs.

U.S. Office for Civil Rights (OCR)

www2.ed.gov/about/offices/list/ocr

Provides information on legal rights, regulations, guidelines, procedures, prevention of school-based harassment, and discriminatory behavior.

Substance Abuse and Mental Health Services Administration (SAMHSA)

www.samhsa.gov

Offers tips on how to start the conversation on bullying and downloadable conversation starter cards, *Make Time to Listen, Take Time to Talk . . . About Bullying.*

Associations

AbilityPath

www.abilitypath.org

A forum for parents and teachers of special needs kids to share tools and resources.

American Civil Liberties Union (ACLU)

www.aclu.org

Fights discrimination in education regarding gender identity and expression, lobbying for passage of the Student Non-Discrimination Act to protect LGBT students in public K–12 schools.

Anti-Defamation League (ADL)

www.adl.org

Promotes justice and fair treatment for all. Its Classroom of Difference program provides anti-bias education and diversity training for grades K–12. Includes a peer-training program.

Collaborative for Academic, Social, and Emotional Learning (CASEL)

www.casel.org

Works to establish social and emotional learning (SEL) as an essential part of education. Provides a map of current SEL standards by state and education level.

Family Voices

www.familyvoices.org

National network of families with special needs children committed to family-centered care for their children.

Gay, Lesbian &
Straight Education Network (GLSEN)

www.glsen.org

Works to ensure that all students are respected regardless of sexual orientation, gender identity, or expression. Materials address teasing, bullying, gender stereotyping, and harassment.

International Bullying Prevention Association

www.stopbullyingworld.org

Supports and enhances quality research-based bullying prevention principles and practices. Presents an annual conference in the United States.

National Network of Partnership Schools

www.csos.jhu.edu/p2000

Brings together schools, districts, states, and organizations to develop programs of parent and community involvement with schools. Offers research-proven tools and professional development. Publishes an annual report, *Promising Partnership Practices*, giving descriptions of collaborations happening around the country.

Parents, Families and Friends
of Lesbians and Gays (PFLAG)

www.pflag.org

Promotes the health and well-being of lesbian, gay, bisexual, and transgender persons, their families, and friends through support, educational materials, and advocacy.

Projects and Programs

Bucket Fillers

www.bucketfillers101.com

Based on a story about invisible buckets in which each of us collect thoughts and experiences that make us feel happy. A teaching program has developed around the awareness of how we can fill each other's buckets through respect and compassion.

BullyBust

www.schoolclimate.org/bullybust

A program launched by the National School Climate Center in 2009 to help students and adults become upstanders. The site offers research-based classroom and schoolwide resources.

Bully Free: It Starts With Me

www.nea.org/home/BullyFreeSchools.html

Campaign developed by the National Education Association that encourages educators and others to pledge to listen and act when a student reports being bullied. The website offers tip sheets and stories.

Bullying Hurts

www.bullyinghurts.com

A mentoring program linking high school students with elementary school students.

Connect for Respect

www.pta.org/bullying

The National Parent Teacher Association provides tools for planning a schoolwide Connect for Respect event to discuss how bullying affects your community and to plan collaborative solutions. Resources and parent tip sheets are available on this site.

Don't Laugh at Me (DLAM)

www.operationrespect.org

Founded by Peter Yarrow, of Peter, Paul, and Mary. Based on conflict resolution curricula developed by the Resolving Conflict Creatively Program of Educators for Social Responsibility. One program for Grades 2–5 and one for Grades 6–8.

e-Buddies

www.ebuddies.org

E-mail pen pal program that connects persons with a developmental disability and their peers who do not have a developmental disability. Provides opportunities for friendships and increased understanding (ages 10 and up).

Eyes on Bullying

www.eyesonbullying.org
Offers a toolkit with strategies, activities, and resources for parents and caregivers of children in programs outside of school. Resources can be used in a classroom as well.

It Gets Better Project

www.itgetsbetter.org
A collection of more than 25,000 user-created videos and stories that support a positive future for LGBT youth going through difficult times.

KiVa Anti-Bullying Program

www.kivakoulu.fi
Program developed by the Finnish Ministry of Education and used in Finnish schools. Encourages onlookers to take action to support the bullied, not the bully. Includes use of a computer game designed to reinforce skills and motivation to change behavior.

Lesson One: The ABCs of Life

www.lessonone.org
A successful academic and social skills intervention being used throughout the country. Program teaches self-confidence, cooperation, problem solving, listening skills, and self-control.

Mix It Up

www.tolerance.org/mix-it-up
Program developed by Teaching Tolerance (Southern Poverty Law Center) to break down social barriers between students in the lunchroom by asking students to connect with someone new over lunch. Activities, lessons, posters, and planning tips available.

Olweus Bullying Prevention Program

www.olweus.org
A comprehensive professional development program pioneered by Dan Olweus 35 years ago in Norway. Provides information on state and U.S. federal laws regarding bullying.

Positive Action

www.positiveaction.net

Program that integrates five building blocks: unit concepts, classroom curriculum, school-climate program, parent, and community programs. Nationally recognized by the U.S. Department of Education What Works Clearinghouse.

Rachel's Challenge

www.rachelschallenge.org

Rachel Scott was killed at Columbine. Rachel's Challenge programs are age-specific for K–12. Program begins with an assembly followed by classroom activities and the formation of Kindness and Compassion clubs. End-of-the-year celebration honors the work students have done to create a healthy school climate.

Special Olympics

www.specialolympics.org

Support of athletes with intellectual disabilities. The Special Olympics continues to build a culture of respect for the participants, and encourages all people to appreciate each other's strengths and differences.

Stomp Out Bullying

www.stompoutbullying.org

A campaign supported by Love Our Children USA and MTV to raise awareness, educate, and advocate through materials and peer mentoring programs in schools. Organizes the Annual World Day of Bullying Prevention—Blue Shirt Day, held on the first Monday in October.

Teaching Tolerance

www.tolerance.org

A project of the Southern Poverty Law Center. Offers classroom activities and teaching kits.

Other Web Resources

Bully Police USA

www.bullypolice.org

A reference site for tracking, evaluating, and comparing anti-bullying laws in every state. Stays current on what is happening around the United States.

Doing What Works

http://dww.ed.gov
Research-based education practices identified by the U.S. Department of Education. Under Comprehensive Support are suggestions for elementary school classroom behavior problems. Site Profiles describe specific school programs that have been successful.

Federal Resources for Educational Excellence

www.free.ed.gov
Links to free curriculum resources from U.S. federal agencies. Many reflect our cultural history.

Find Youth Info

www.findyouthinfo.gov
Provides a searchable database of evidence-based programs that prevent or reduce problem behaviors in young people.

McRel Compendium of Standards and Benchmarks

www.mcrel.org/standards-benchmarks
A searchable free online version of *Content Knowledge: A Compendium of Standards and Benchmarks for K–12 Education*, a database of standards. Also provides a link to Common Core Standards to help you document the value added with STAND TALL.

National Bullying Prevention Center

www.pacer.org/bullying
Videos, tool kits, and lesson plans to address bullying.

No Name-Calling Week

www.nonamecallingweek.org
Ideas and resources for participating in No Name-Calling Week in your school.

Pacer Center's Kids Against Bullying

www.pacerkidsagainstbullying.org
   Website for kids. Videos, webisodes, contests, games, and information about how to respond when someone is bullied.

Sprigeo

www.sprigeo.com
   Online bully incident reporting system for tracking and documenting bullying incidents. Also offers an Onsite Bully Prevention Program for middle schools and a robust, informative website.

Stop Bullying.gov

www.stopbullying.gov
   Premier clearinghouse for federal agencies to consolidate bully prevention information and resources.

Stop Bullying Speak Up (Cartoon Network)

www.stopbullyingspeakup.com
   Resources for kids and parents, including contests and online videos.

Tangled Ball

www.tangledball.blogspot.com
   Susan S. Raisch's blog keeps you updated on programs and resources that address issues of bullying and online safety.

TIPS Interactive Homework
(Teachers Involve Parents in Schoolwork)

www.csos.jhu.edu/p2000/tips/subject.htm
   The National Network of Partnership Schools at Johns Hopkins University offers sample activities and blank forms for designing homework projects that involve family in educational activities to complement classroom learning.

Books

This book list is divided into books for children and books for teachers or parents.

The children's books cover a range of topics to expand your students' world view, teach them about other cultures, and provide ideas on how to stand up in bullying situations.

You might choose a book a week to read in your classroom in order to keep the STAND TALL discussion alive throughout the year. Scan through the list for books that fit your classroom, such as the story of the girl who recognizes that a fellow student with a mental disability needs support; or the true story of Sadako, a Japanese girl in Hiroshima who develops leukemia, which inspires students worldwide to fold cranes; or the story of Gita, a recent immigrant to the United States from India who finds help for her homesickness in sharing the Festival of Lights traditions with her new best friend.

A few how-to books are included among the books for children. These are written specifically for children in the Grade 4–6 range.

The books for teachers and parents offer insight for adults on how to understand, prevent, and respond thoughtfully to situations that reflect bullying behavior.

For Children

50 Cent. (2011). *Playground: The mostly true story of a former bully*. New York, NY: Razorbill.

> Thirteen-year-old Butterball doesn't have much going for him. But that's not why he beat up Maurice on the playground. Inspired by 50 Cent's own adolescence, this is the hard-hitting and inspirational story of the redemption of a bully.

Beckwith, K. (2005). *Playing war*. Gardiner, ME: Tilbury House.

> Children learn from a new neighbor that war is not a game to someone who has experienced a real war (ages 8 to 12).

Bridges, R. (2001). *Through my eyes*. New York, NY: Scholastic.

> At 6, Ruby was the first black student to attend William Frantz Public School in New Orleans (1960). Written in her own words decades later (ages 8 to 12).

Bromley, A. C. (2010). *The lunch thief.* Gardiner, ME: Tilbury House.

When Rafael sees another student steal his lunch, instead of reacting with anger, he takes time to find out why Kevin is stealing food. Then Rafael offers a solution (ages 7 to 12).

Clements, A. (2001). *Jake Drake, bully buster.* New York, NY: Simon & Schuster.

Jake decides to stop Link Baxter's reign of terror. In the process, he finds out Link is a nicer person than he expected (ages 7 to 10).

Coerr, E. (2003). *Mieko and the fifth treasure.* New York, NY: Puffin.

Mieko's hand is injured during the bombing of Nagasaki, so she can no longer do calligraphy or art. Sent to a new school, she is taunted by some classmates, but with the support of a special friendship and her family, she finds the fifth treasure, "beauty in the heart," and begins to paint again (ages 7 to 11).

Coerr, E. (2005). *Sadako and the thousand paper cranes.* New York, NY: Puffin.

The true story of a young Japanese girl in Hiroshima who develops leukemia from exposure to the atom bomb. Sadako wants to fold 1,000 paper cranes before she dies, but completes only 644. Her classmates fold the remaining cranes so that she can be buried with 1,000 cranes (ages 9 to 12).

Cohn, J. (2000). *The Christmas menorahs: How a town fought hate.* Morton Grove, IL: A. Whitman.

Recounts a true event in Billings, Montana, when a rock was thrown through the bedroom window where a young boy had his menorah displayed. In response, many people of Billings put menorahs in their windows (ages 7 to 11).

Collard, S. (2005). *Dog sense.* Atlanta, GA: Peachtree.

Having moved from California to Montana, Guy is targeted by a bully named Brad. When Guy enters his dog Streak into a Frisbee contest, he decides to make a bargain with Brad because Guy's grandfather has explained that the best victory is win-win (ages 10 to 14).

Cooper, S. (2005). *Speak up and get along.* Minneapolis, MN: Free Spirit.

Tools for expressing yourself, ending arguments and fights, and ways to resolve conflicts and get along with others (ages 9 to 12).

Curtis, C. P. (2000). *The Watsons go to Birmingham—1963.* New York, NY: Bantam Books.

> An African American family takes a trip from Michigan to Alabama in 1963, arriving in Birmingham just as the civil rights movement events take place (ages 9 to 14).

Emerson, K. (2008). *Carlos is gonna get it.* New York, NY: Arthur A. Levine Books.

> Trina and her middle school classmates recognize that Carlos is strange. Carlos has a mental disability. When her classmates plan to play a trick on him, Trina is emotionally caught between peer pressure and helping Carlos. The prank goes awry, and all must face the consequences of their actions (ages 9 to 12).

Estes, E. (2004). *The hundred dresses.* New York, NY: Sandpiper Harcourt.

> Ridiculed by her classmates for wearing the same dress every day, Wanda Petronski tells them that she has 100 dresses at home. She is teased relentlessly until the family decides it is better to move away, and her classmates realize what they have done (ages 6 to 10).

Fox, D., & Beane, A. L. (2009). *Good-bye bully machine.* Minneapolis, MN: Free Spirit.

> While initially comparing the bully to a cold scary machine, this story provides insight into what makes bullies act the way they do and encourages kids to take a stand against bully behavior (ages 8 to 12).

Friesen, G. (2000). *Men of stone.* Toronto, Ontario, Canada: Kids Can Press.

> Fifteen-year-old Ben is harassed by Claude after Claude discovers that Ben takes ballet. It's finally Ben's great-aunt Frieda who inspires him to be true to his talent when she describes how she stood up to harassment by Stalin's agents in her town in Russia (ages 8 to 16).

Gatto, P., & De Angelis, J. (2004). *Milton's dilemma.* Houston, TX: Providence.

> Ten-year-old Milton becomes the target of bullies in his new school. He vows revenge with the help of a magical gnome, but

soon finds that revenge isn't as pleasant as he had hoped (ages 6 to 10).

Gilmore, R. (2000). *Lights for Gita.* Gardiner, ME: Tilbury House.

A recent immigrant from India, Gita prepares for the Hindu festival of lights, Divali. An ice storm knocks out the power, but while sharing the holiday with her best friend, she finds that the candlelight brightens the darkness around her and within her (ages 8 to 12).

Gilmore, R. (2001). *Roses for Gita.* Gardiner, ME: Tilbury House.

Gita finds the path to a friendship that overcomes differences in age and culture through a shared love of music and flowers (ages 8 to 12).

Gilmore, R. (2002). *A gift for Gita.* Gardiner, ME: Tilbury House.

When Gita's father gets a job offer that would take them back to India, Gita discovers that the friendships she has made in her new community have made Canada feel like home to her (ages 8 to 12).

Green, S. (2010). *Don't pick on me.* Oakland, CA: Instant Help Books.

A workbook with confidence-building activities that address teasing, gossip, name-calling, cyberbullying, and other forms of harassment (ages 9 to 12).

Hoose, P. (2001). *We were there too! Young people in U.S. history.* New York, NY: Farrar, Straus and Giroux.

Stories of youth who have impacted U.S. history (ages 10 to 14).

Hoose, P. (2002). *It's our world too: Young people who are making a difference: How they do it—How you can too.* New York, NY: Farrar, Straus and Giroux.

Book of tools for taking action to bring about social change. Companion to the book *We Were There Too!* (ages 10 and up).

Hoose, P. (2009). *Claudette Colvin: Twice toward justice.* New York, NY: Farrar, Straus and Giroux.

At 15, Claudette Colvin was arrested for challenging segregation laws in Montgomery, Alabama. At 16 she challenged these laws in a landmark court case that led to the integration of Montgomery's buses (ages 10 to 15).

Houtman, J. (2010). *The reinvention of Edison Thomas.* Honesdale, PA: Front Street.

> Nasty pranks are played on Eddie, who doesn't easily recognize social cues. His avid interest in science, however, wins him some true friendships. His friends help him recognize bullying behavior and he figures out how to stand up to those who are bullying him (ages 10 to 14).

Howe, J. (2003). *The misfits.* New York, NY: Simon & Schuster.

> Four seventh graders form a party to run for student council to take a stand against name-calling and show appreciation for diversity (ages 10 to 14).

Howling, E. (2008). *Drive.* Toronto, Ontario, Canada: J. Lorimer.

> Jake is a budding golf pro who doesn't have the money for clubs or course membership and is bullied by the younger members. When a pro offers to teach him, he must stand up to the bullies (ages 8 to 13).

Jarman, J. (2000). *Hangman.* London, UK: Collins.

> Toby is embarrassed to be friends with Danny, but when bullies go too far, Toby finds he must choose sides to possibly save a life (ages 9 to 12).

Kaye, C. B. (2007). *A kid's guide to hunger and homelessness: How to take action!* Minneapolis, MN: Free Spirit.

> Guides students in developing service projects to address the needs of their community (ages 9 to 12).

Kimmel, H. (2007). *Kaline Klattermaster's tree house.* New York, NY: Atheneum.

> Kaline's father has disappeared, his mom is a little crazy, and bullies are harassing him. He goes to his neighbor Mr. Putnaminsky for advice. Kaline learns to stand up and be true to himself (ages 8 to 11).

Knight, M. B. (2003). *Who belongs here?* Gardiner, ME: Tilbury House.

> Nary arrives in the United States with his family as refugees from Cambodia. When some classmates suggest he go back, that raises the question of whose families, besides Native Americans, didn't migrate here from another country (ages 8 to 12).

Korman, G. (2010). *Radio fifth grade.* New York, NY: Scholastic.

Fifth grader Benji coproduces a radio show at a local station. Brad, known as the school bully, asks to read his stories on the program. No one has the nerve to tell him how bad the stories are. Eventually Benji must confront Brad and tell him the truth. He is surprised by Brad's response (ages 9 to 12).

Koss, A. G. (2006). *Poison ivy.* New Milford, CT: Roaring Brook Press.

Eight first-person narrators give different versions of the same event and insights into human nature (ages 10 to 15).

Jakubiak, D. (2010). *Smart kid's guide to online bullying.* New York, NY: PowerKids Press.

Explains to elementary school kids what to watch for and how to stay safe online (ages 7 to 11).

Lombard, J. (2006). *Drita, my homegirl.* New York, NY: G. P. Putnam's Sons.

Ten-year-old Drita, a refugee from Kosovo, is interviewed by Maxie, an African American classmate. In the process of Maxie interviewing Drita for a social studies report, each girl develops unexpected insight into the life of the other (ages 9 to 12).

Lord, C. (2008). *Rules.* New York, NY: Scholastic.

Catherine has created rules about what is "normal" for her younger brother David, who is autistic. Summer friendships with a new neighbor and a paraplegic boy help her to redefine normal with a greater respect for differences (ages 9 to 12).

Ludwig, T. (2005). *My secret bully.* Berkeley, CA: Ten Speed Press.

Friends since kindergarten, Monica finds that Katie has started to embarrass and exclude her when they are with classmates. Monica's mom helps her identify ways to respond and regain her confidence when Katie treats her badly (ages 5 to 11).

Ludwig, T. (2010). *Confessions of a former bully.* Berkeley, CA: Tricycle Press.

After bullying a friend on the playground, Kate meets with the principal to discuss the effects of bullying. This book journals her experience (ages 8 to 12).

Maguire, G. (2002). *Three rotten eggs.* New York, NY: Clarion Books.

A Hamlet Chronicles adventure, this book focuses on an annual Spring Egg Hunt competition gone awry. Three genetically altered eggs hatch fire-breathing chicks. The winning class is disqualified for cheating and must all work together (including the bully and his friends, who are responsible for the eggs) to redeem themselves (ages 9 to 12).

McCain, B. R. (2001). *Nobody knew what to do: A story about bullying.* Morton Grove, IL: A. Whitman.

A student goes to the teacher for help when he sees his classmate Ray being bullied. With help from his teacher, the student and other classmates stand up to the bullies to stop them from bothering Ray (ages 6 to 9).

McCloud, C. (2011). *Growing up with a bucket full of happiness: Three rules for a happier life.* Northville, MI: Ferne Press.

Based on the concept that each person has an imaginary bucket, which contains a person's sense of well-being and happiness, this book delves into the importance of respecting differences, learning resilience, finding courage, and expressing compassion (ages 9 to 12).

McIntyre, T. (2003). *The behavior survival guide for kids: How to make good choices and stay out of trouble.* Minneapolis, MN: Free Spirit.

Written for children with behavioral problems. Offers strategies for dealing with problems and choosing better ways to respond (ages 9 to 12).

McNamee, G. (2001). *Nothing wrong with a three-legged dog.* New York, NY: Yearling.

Keath, a white fourth-grade student in a mostly African American school, and his biracial friend Lynda love dogs. Lynda's dog Leftovers is a three-legged beagle with one ear. Leftovers was abandoned by his owners. As the story progresses, Keath learns to look beyond superficial physical attributes (ages 9 to 12).

Mead, A. (2002). *Junebug and the reverend.* New York, NY: Yearling.

Ten-year-old Junebug moves from the projects to live near an assisted living facility where his mother is a supervisor. He must walk the aged Reverend Ashford every morning, then deal with the bullies at school. He learns life lessons from the Reverend and forms friendships that help him develop as a member of his new community (ages 9 to 12).

Millman, I. (2002). *Moses goes to a concert*. New York, NY: Farrar, Straus and Giroux.

Moses and his classmates are hearing impaired. However, they can feel vibrations, so their teacher takes them to a concert where they hold balloons to feel the music and they meet a percussionist who is deaf (ages 5 to 10).

Mills, C. (2000). *Lizzie at last*. New York, NY: Farrar, Straus and Giroux.

Lizzie decides that seventh grade is the year she will fit in and be popular, so she discards her flowing thrift store dresses and hides her intelligence. It works, but she realizes that she doesn't need to play by the popular girls' rules to find friendship (ages 9 to 12).

Morrison, T. (2004). *Remember: The journey to school integration*. Boston, MA: Houghton Mifflin.

Using archival photos, Toni Morrison develops a story around a group of schoolchildren photographed during the period leading up to and during school integration (ages 10 to 17).

Moss, M. (2006). *Amelia's bully survival guide*. New York, NY: Simon & Schuster.

After spending winter break at Space Camp, Amelia returns to her fifth-grade class with the confidence to stand up to the bully who has been picking on her (ages 9 to 12).

Moss, P. (2004). *Say something*. Gardiner, ME: Tilbury House.

The story of a young girl who feels sorry for students who are bullied but doesn't intervene. When she is bullied and no one comes to her aid, she realizes why it is important to step in to help stop the bullying (ages 8 to 12).

Moss, P. (2010). *One of us*. Gardiner, ME: Tilbury House.

New to her elementary school, Roberta arrives after the cliques have formed. She moves from group to group in search of where she fits. Then she finds the group where each child is different and appreciated for those differences (ages 8 to 12).

Moss, P., & Tardiff, D. D. (2007). *Our friendship rules.* Gardiner, ME: Tilbury House.

> Caught between the popular girls and her best friend, Alexandra chooses to be with the popular girls. But when she sees that she has hurt her best friend, she realizes the value of that friendship (ages 8 to 12).

Murphy, B. B. (2002). *Miguel lost and found in the Palace.* Santa Fe, NM: Museum of New Mexico Press.

> Miguel is the son of undocumented immigrants. After some traumatic family experiences, he moves with his mom and sisters to Santa Fe, New Mexico. There, he is intimidated and chased by a gang of bullies. While hiding in the Palace of the Governors, he learns about and finds pride in his Mexican heritage (ages 9 to 12).

Myers, C. (2000). *Wings.* New York, NY: Scholastic Press.

> Ikarus, a young boy with wings, is treated badly for being different. He continues to fly but begins to show signs of dejection, resting on top of a building with a group of pigeons who "don't make fun of people." At that point the shy young narrator calls out to defend him to the onlookers and points out the unique beauty of Ikarus's wings (ages 7 and up).

Nikola-Lisa, W. (2006). *How we are smart.* New York, NY: Lee & Low.

> Shows examples of different ways of being smart by exhibiting the work of 12 people famous for different types of work (ages 9 to 12).

Petrillo, G. (2009). *Keep your ear on the ball.* Gardiner, ME: Tilbury House.

> Davey is blind but very independent. When he has difficulty playing kickball, the other students are surprised. Together they figure out how to help Davey succeed and learn the value of interdependence (ages 8 to 12).

Phillips, A. A. (2007). *If you believe in mermaids—don't tell.* Indianapolis, IN: Dog Ear.

> When Todd chooses a summer nature camp over the sports camp his dad wants him to attend, Todd finds the courage to accept and become confident about his own gender identity (ages 9 to 12).

Romaine, T. (2001). *Bullies are a pain in the brain.* Minneapolis, MN: Free Spirit.

> Self-help book for kids who want tips on how to respond to bullying (ages 8 to 12).

Roy, J. (2009). *Max Quigley, technically not a bully.* Boston, MA: Houghton Mifflin Harcourt.

> Max excels at making trouble, especially for Triffin, who is one of the smart kids. Max doesn't see himself as a bully until he realizes that is how others see him. When Max surprisingly comes to Triffin's aid during an incident, the reader sees the possibility of a future friendship (ages 9 to 12).

Russo, M. (2005). *Always remember me: How one family survived World War II.* New York, NY: Atheneum.

> Holocaust survival story of the author's grandmother, mother, and two aunts. True stories of four brave women, told to the author by her grandmother at the dinner table after their Sunday dinners (ages 8 to 12).

Savageau, C. (2006). *Muskrat will be swimming.* Gardiner, ME: Tilbury House.

> Jeannie is referred to as a lake rat by other students because she lives in the shanty town by the lake. Her Native American grandfather helps her feel her connection to the lake and her own identity (ages 9 to 12).

Schrock, J. W. (2008). *Give a goat.* Gardiner, ME: Tilbury House.

> A fifth-grade class, inspired by the story of the gift of a goat to a Ugandan girl, decides to raise money to buy a goat for a family through the Heifer International program (ages 9 to 12).

Spinelli, J. (2004). *Crash.* New York, NY: Dell Laurel-Leaf.

> Seventh grader Crash has been tormenting Penn since they were 6. Family events lead Crash to a new level of sensitivity, compassion, and appreciation for Penn (ages 8 to 12).

Stolz, M., & Shortall, L. (2006). *The bully of Barkham Street.* New York, NY: HarperCollins.

> An 11-year-old bully named Martin provides insight into what leads a person to become a bully and how he or she can meet those needs in healthier ways (ages 8 to 12).

Stones, R. (2005). *Don't pick on me: How to handle bullying*. London, UK: Piccadilly Press.

> Discussion of why children are bullied, why some become bullies, and what they can do to stop the bullying (ages 8 and up).

Uchida, Y. (2005). *Journey to Topaz*. Berkeley, CA: Heyday Books.

> Chronicles the lives of Yuki, a 12-year-old Japanese American girl, and her family when they are sent from Berkeley to a World War II internment camp in Utah (ages 9 to 12).

Uhlberg, M. (2006). *Dad, Jackie and me*. Atlanta, GA: Peachtree Press.

> A young boy with a father who is deaf follows the career of Jackie Robinson. The son learns about discrimination and feels respect for Robinson and also for his father (ages 7 to 11).

Van Draanen, W. (2004). *Shredderman: Secret identity*. New York, NY: Knopf.

> Small but smart, fifth-grade student Nolan is relentlessly bullied by Bubba Bixby. For a class project, Nolan creates Shredderman, a web superhero. Shredderman's adventures are based on Nolan's experiences with Bubba (ages 8 to 12).

Verdick, E., & Lisovskis, M. (2003). *How to take the grrrr out of anger*. Minneapolis, MN: Free Spirit.

> While anger is a part of life, violence is not acceptable. This book describes healthy ways to express anger (ages 9 to 12).

Wesselman, H. (2004). *Little Ruth Reddingford and the wolf: An old tale*. Bellevue, WA: Illumination Arts.

> Two bullies follow Ruth on her way to her grandma's condo. Ruth finds that with the help of her Hopi grandmother and her spirit guardian, the white wolf, she is empowered to stand up to the bullies (ages 4 to 10).

Wilson, J. (2006). *Bad girls*. New York, NY: Delacorte Press.

> First the bully girls pick on Mandy, then her best friend joins them. When Tanya moves into her neighborhood, they make friends and Mandy learns to appreciate individuality (ages 9 to 12).

Wolf, B. (2003). *Coming to America: A Muslim family's story*. New York, NY: Lee & Low Books.

The Mahmoud family arrives in New York from Egypt. Becoming part of their new community involves learning a new language, finding appropriate jobs, experiencing homesickness, and building friendships (ages 7 to 11).

Woodson, J. (2001). *The other side.* New York, NY: G. P. Putnam's Sons.

Clover and Anna live on different sides of the fence that separates the white people in their town from their African American neighbors. The friends decide to sit on top of the fence to visit with each other (ages 5 and up).

Yee, L. (2011). *Warp speed.* New York, NY: Arthur A. Levine.

Marley is a *Star Trek* fan who frequently has to deal with bullies. Marley learns to stand up for himself, appreciate differences, and find that even bullies are not two-dimensional people (ages 9 to 12).

Yep, L. (2000). *Cockroach cooties.* New York, NY: Hyperion.

Brothers Teddy and Bobby discover that Arnie, the school bully, is afraid of cockroaches. They also discover the reason for his fear and understand his anger (ages 8 to 11).

Zimmer, T. V. (2007). *Reaching for sun.* New York, NY: Bloomsbury Children's Books.

Josie has cerebral palsy. Meeting a new neighbor, she learns the value of friendship (ages 10 to 14).

For Teachers and Parents

Anderson, S. (2011). *No more bystanders = no more bullies.* Thousand Oaks, CA: Corwin.

Guide to transforming school culture from passive to proactive.

Barton, E. A. (2006). *Bully prevention.* Thousand Oaks, CA: Corwin.

Psychology of bullies and guidelines for intervention.

Beaudoin, N., & Taylor, M. (2009). *Responding to the culture of bullying and disrespect.* Thousand Oaks, CA: Corwin.

Guide to positive responses to misbehavior, encouraging greater responsibility and respect.

Borba, M. (2009). *The big book of parenting solutions: 101 answers to your everyday challenges and wildest worries.* San Francisco, CA: Jossey-Bass.

> Guide for dealing with child behavior challenges for parents of kids ages 3 to 13. Includes but is not limited to bullying behavior.

Bowles, N. E., & Rosenthal, M. (Eds.). (2001). *Cootie shots: Theatrical inoculations against bigotry for kids, parents, and teachers.* New York, NY: Theater Communications Group.

> A collection of plays, poems, and songs that address bias and prejudice. Developed by a group of educators, parents, and teens.

Breakstone, S., Dreiblatt, M., & Dreiblatt, K. (2008). *How to stop bullying and social aggression.* Thousand Oaks, CA: Corwin.

> Elementary-grade activities that teach empathy, friendship, and respect.

Brunner, J. M., & Lewis, D. K. (2006). *School house bullies (DVD and facilitator's guide).* Thousand Oaks, CA: Corwin.

> Vignettes of bullying behaviors that occur in K–12 schools. Print guide develops ways to prevent or defuse these behaviors.

Burke, K. (2008). *What to do with the kid who . . .* Thousand Oaks, CA: Corwin.

> Guide to developing cooperation, self-discipline, and responsibility in the classroom.

Colorosa, B. (2003). *The bully, the bullied, and the bystander: From preschool to high school: How parents and teachers can help break the cycle of violence.* New York, NY: HarperResource.

> Special focus on how to respond when someone else is being bullied.

Ferlazzo, L., & Hammond, L. (2009). *Building parent engagement in schools.* Columbus, OH: Linworth Books.

> Ways to engage parents and the community in active participation, building on the needs, strengths, and knowledge of the community.

Field, J. E., Kolbert, J. B., Crothers, L. M., & Hughes, T. L. (2009). *Understanding girl bullying and what to do about it: Strategies to help heal the divide.* Thousand Oaks, CA: Corwin.

> Helps professionals heal the divide between girls by giving them the tools to work through their problems thoughtfully and constructively.

Freedman, J. (2002). *Easing the teasing: Helping your child cope with name-calling, ridicule, and verbal bullying.* Chicago, IL: Contemporary Books.

> Strategies for responding to teasing and verbal bullying in ways that can help defuse the aggression (ages 8 to 12).

Glasgow, N. A., & Whitney, P. J. (2009). *What successful schools do to involve families: 55 partnership strategies.* Thousand Oaks, CA: Corwin.

> Strategies for bridging the gap between school and home.

Gootman, M. E. (2010). *The caring teacher's guide to discipline: Helping students learn self-control, responsibility, and respect, K–6* (2nd ed.). Thousand Oaks, CA: Corwin.

> Help students deal with anger, correct misbehavior, and prevent misunderstandings.

Hinduja, S., & Patchin, J. W. (2008). *Bullying beyond the schoolyard: Preventing and responding to cyberbullying.* Thousand Oaks, CA: Corwin.

> Helps educators confront technology-based aggression and establish safe, responsible use of computers and the Internet.

Horne, A. M., Bartolomucci, C. L., & Newman-Carlson, D. (2003). *Bully busters: A teacher's manual for helping bullies, victims, and bystanders.* Champaign, IL: Research Press.

> Guide for teachers of kindergarten through fifth grade. Activities to strengthen a student's self-confidence and ways to encourage parents to partner with educators to reduce and prevent bullying.

Kaye, C. B. (2010). *The complete guide to service learning: Proven practical ways to engage students in civic responsibility, academic curriculum, and social action.* Minneapolis, MN: Free Spirit.

> Ideas for K–12 service learning projects that link to classroom curriculum.

Mah, R. (2009). *Getting beyond bullying and exclusion, preK–5: Empowering children in inclusive classrooms.* Thousand Oaks, CA: Corwin.

> Discusses the sensitivity and expertise that educators need to help children with special needs become more resilient and experience success at school.

McGrath, M. J. (2006). *School bullying: Tools for avoiding harm and liability.* Thousand Oaks, CA: Corwin.

> Legally based, ethically sound approaches to dealing with and preventing bullying in schools.

Myers, J. J., McCaw, D. S., & Hemphill, L. S. (2011). *Responding to cyber bullying: An action tool for school leaders.* Thousand Oaks, CA: Corwin.

> Clear guidance for honoring free expression while providing a safe learning environment.

Osborne, A. G., Jr., & Russo, C. J. (2011). *The legal rights and responsibilities of teachers: Issues of employment and instruction.* Thousand Oaks, CA: Corwin.

> Everything teachers need to know about education law.

Preble, B., & Gordon, R. (2011). *Transforming school climate and learning: Beyond bullying and compliance.* Thousand Oaks, CA: Corwin.

> How to create a respectful culture using a collaborative action research model.

Roberts, W. B., Jr. (2005). *Bullying from both sides: Strategic interventions for working with bullies and victims.* Thousand Oaks, CA: Corwin.

> How to work effectively with the bullies as well as the victims.

Roberts, W. B., Jr. (2007). *Working with the parents of bullies and victims.* Thousand Oaks, CA: Corwin.

> Strategies for conversations and interventions with even the most persistent or resistant parents.

Sapon-Shevin, M. (2010). *Because we can change the world: A practical guide to building cooperative, inclusive classroom communities.* Thousand Oaks, CA: Corwin.

> Structuring democratic classrooms as models of diversity, cooperation, and inclusion.

Savage, D., & Miller, T. (2011). *It gets better.* New York, NY: Dutton.

Essays and testimonials from celebrities, political leaders, and everyday people to help LGBT youth cope with bullying and believe in a positive future for themselves.

Sullivan, K. (2010). *The anti-bullying handbook.* Thousand Oaks, CA: Corwin.

A clear overview of what we understand about bullying and how to use collaborative and restorative justice techniques.

Trolley, B. C., & Hanel, C. (2010). *Cyber kids, cyber bullying, cyber balance.* Thousand Oaks, CA: Corwin.

Uses real-life scenarios to describe how to teach kids about the benefits and danger of online activities.

Winslade, J., & Williams, M. (2011). *Safe and peaceful schools: Addressing conflict and eliminating violence.* Thousand Oaks, CA: Corwin.

How to teach students to deal with conflict constructively and reduce the need for disciplinary action.

Wiseman, R. (2002). *Queen bees and wannabes: Helping your daughter survive cliques, gossip, boyfriends and other realities of adolescence.* New York, NY: Crown.

Helps adolescents and the adults who love them navigate Girl World from fifth grade through adulthood. Includes perspective on social networking technology and cyberbullying.

References

Angelou, M. (1993). *Wouldn't take nothing for my journey now.* New York, NY: Random House.

Bernstein, L. (1963, November 25). *Tribute to John F. Kennedy.* Speech made at United Jewish Appeal benefit, New York, NY.

Conoley, C. W., & Conoley, J. C. (2009). *Positive psychology and family therapy: Creative techniques and practical tools for guiding change and enhancing growth.* Hoboken, NJ: John Wiley & Sons.

Collaborative for Academic, Social, and Emotional Learning. (2011). *Benefits of social and emotional learning.* Retrieved from http://casel.org/wp-content/uploads/2011/04/benefits.png

Hinduja, S., & Patchin, J. W. (2009). *Bullying beyond the schoolyard: Preventing and responding to cyberbullying.* Thousand Oaks, CA: Corwin.

Kaiser Family Foundation. (2011). *Talking with kids (and parents): A new public information partnership with Nickelodeon.* Retrieved from http://www.kff.org/mediapartnerships/3105-index.cfm

Koebcke, D. (2008). *A bystander leader approach to safer schools: Team LEAD sample contract.* Retrieved from http://www.bystanderlead.com/APDFsTL08/SampleContractA.pdf

Leonard, G. B. (1987). *Education and ecstasy.* Berkeley, CA: North Atlantic Books.

Mah, R. (2007). *The working it out plan.* Retrieved from http://www.ronaldmah.com/page20.htm#THE WORKING IT OUT PLAN

Mah, R. (2009). *Getting beyond bullying and exclusion.* Thousand Oaks, CA: Corwin.

Naylor, P. R. (1994). *The king of the playground.* New York, NY: Aladdin Paperbacks.

Obama, B. (2008, May 28). *What's possible for our children.* Speech given at Mapleton Expeditionary School of the Arts, Thornton, CO. Retrieved from http://www.denverpost.com/ci_9405199

O'Toole, J., & Burton, B. (2010). *Acting against bullying: Using drama and peer teaching to reduce bullying.* Retrieved from http://www.education.com/reference/article/act-against-reduce-bullying-peer-teaching

Roberts, W. B., Jr. (2006). *Bullying from both sides: Strategic interventions for working with bullies and victims.* Thousand Oaks, CA: Corwin.

Sapon-Shevin, M. (2010). *Because we can change the world: A practical guide to building cooperative, inclusive classroom communities.* Thousand Oaks, CA: Corwin.

U.S. Department of Education, Office for Civil Rights. (2010a). *Dear colleague letter.* Retrieved from http://www2.ed.gov/about/offices/list/ocr/letters/colleague-201010.html

U.S. Department of Education, Office for Civil Rights. (2010b). *Guidance targeting harassment outlines local and federal responsibility.* Retrieved from http://www.ed.gov/news/press-releases/guidance-targeting-harassment-outlines-local-and-federal-responsibility

U.S. Department of Education, Office for Civil Rights. (2011, July 1). *Departments of Justice and Education Reach Agreement with Tehachapi Public Schools to Resolve Harassment Allegations.* Retrieved from http://www.ed.gov/news/press-releases/departments-justice-and-education-reach-agreement-tehachapi-calif-public-schools

U.S. Department of Health and Human Services. (n.d.). *Recognizing the warning signs.* Retrieved from http://www.stopbullying.gov/topics/warning_signs/

Index

Note: page numbers followed by "f," "t," and "b" indicate figures, tables, and boxes, respectively.

CORWIN
A SAGE Company

The Corwin logo—a raven striding across an open book—represents the union of courage and learning. Corwin is committed to improving education for all learners by publishing books and other professional development resources for those serving the field of PreK–12 education. By providing practical, hands-on materials, Corwin continues to carry out the promise of its motto: **"Helping Educators Do Their Work Better."**